Conservation Treatment Procedures

CONSERVATION TREATMENT PROCEDURES

A Manual of Step-by-Step Procedures for the Maintenance and Repair of Library Materials

SECOND EDITION

Carolyn Clark Morrow and Carole Dyal

Photographs by Todd C. Matus

1986

Libraries Unlimited, Inc.   Littleton, Colorado

LIBRARIES UNLIMITED, INC.
P.O. Box 263
Littleton, Colorado 80160-0263

Library of Congress Cataloging-in-Publication Data

Morrow, Carolyn Clark.
    Conservation treatment procedures.

    Bibliography: p. 221.
    1. Library materials--Conservation and restoration--
Handbooks, manuals, etc. I. Dyal, Carole. II. Matus,
Todd. III. Title.
Z701.M545   1986   025.7   86-20948
ISBN 0-87287-437-0

The paper used in this publication meets the minimum requirements of American National Standard for Information Sciences — Permanence of Paper for Printed Library Materials, ANSI Z39.48-1984. ∞™

Libraries Unlimited books are bound with Type II nonwoven material that meets and exceeds National Association of State Textbook Administrators' Type II nonwoven material specifications Class A through E.

Contents

Preface to the Second Edition vii

1—INTRODUCTION 1
   The Conservation Function 1
   Understanding Treatment Options 4
      Book Repair 4
      Maintenance 6
      Protective Enclosure 9
   Organizing and Supervising the Conservation Workshop 11
      Priorities and Decision Making 11
      Training and Productivity 12

2—BOOK REPAIR PROCEDURES 15
   Tightening the Hinges of a Case-bound Book 15
      Illustrated 16
   Replacing a Torn Endsheet 19
      Illustrated 21
   New Bookcloth Spine with Mounted Original Spine 30
      Illustrated 32
   Recasing Using the Original Cover 44
      Illustrated 46
   Lining the Spine of an Original Cover 57
      Illustrated 59
   Reattaching Loose Sections 65
      Illustrated 67
   New Cover 69
      Illustrated 73

3—MAINTENANCE PROCEDURES 81
   Pamphlet Binding 81
      Illustrated 83
   Paperback Reinforcement 93
      Illustrated 94
   Pressboard Reinforcement of Paperbacks 99
      Illustrated 100

Mending with Japanese Paper and Starch Paste 105
  Illustrated 107
Mending with Heat-Set Tissue 113
  Illustrated 114

4—PROTECTIVE ENCLOSURE PROCEDURES 117
Polyester Film Encapsulation 117
  Illustrated 119
Simple Portfolio 123
  Illustrated 125
Phase Box 132
  Illustrated 135
Double-Tray Box 142
  Illustrated 145
Polyester Book 164
  Illustrated 167

Appendix 1   **Decision-Making Checklist for Book Repair** 177
Appendix 2   **Developing In-House Capabilities: Profiles of Four Hypothetical Libraries** 179
Appendix 3   **Equipment, Tools, Supplies, and Suppliers** 182
Appendix 4   **Dexterity Test** 210
Appendix 5   **Glossary** 212

SELECTED BIBLIOGRAPHY 221

Preface to the Second Edition

The first edition of this manual was published four years ago on the eve of a period of expanding preservation activity in libraries large and small. Staff who had attended preservation conferences returned enthusiastic ... and armed with information to justify new preservation initiatives. This increased awareness also increased the need for guidance in developing specific preservation routines where none existed before. The first edition was written to fill a crucial part of that void by describing a series of simple conservation procedures to physically maintain and protect book and paper collections.

The second edition incorporates extensive changes and additions. Eleven of the twelve original procedures were completely revised and six totally new procedures added. Two hundred thirty-eight photographs were taken to illustrate the procedures, including another nineteen showing equipment and tools. Four years between editions is a long time in an expanding field such as library conservation, and the changes made reflect improved techniques and the use of new supplies and equipment. The six new procedures expand the manual's coverage, resulting in a more complete tool designed to address the practical conservation problems libraries face each day.

Perhaps most important, the second edition is a team effort of a preservation librarian and a conservator to develop a guide reflecting the point of view and needs of both. Conservation staff will find detailed explanations of procedures, lists of supplies and equipment, and extensive illustrations. Librarians will find guides to determining the scope of a conservation program suited to a particular library collection, and to measuring the quality and suitability of ongoing conservation activities.

Chapter 1 discusses the role of conservation activities in libraries and how they can best be organized and supervised. Each category of conservation treatment options—book repair, maintenance, and protective enclosure—is described and analyzed from an administrative and decision-making perspective. Chapters 2 through 4 give detailed explanations of the procedures. The appendices provide additional information to help libraries establish conservation programs, including a decision-making checklist, a description of four hypothetical libraries and their conservation strategies, a list of equipment and suppliers, and a dexterity test for prospective conservation staff. The glossary explains terms used in the manual and a selected, annotated bibliography suggests additional readings.

This joint effort was conceived and begun when the authors worked together at Morris Library, Southern Illinois University. Our sincere appreciation is extended to the university and especially to Dean Kenneth G. Peterson for creating a supportive atmosphere for research and professional development. Recognition is also due to the many student assistants who helped test and refine the procedures.

Carolyn Clark Morrow
Carole Dyal

1
Introduction

THE CONSERVATION FUNCTION

The need for conservation and repair of library materials is determined by their physical and chemical composition, the environment in which they are stored, and their history of use and abuse.

The inherent physical composition and structure of an item, along with the permanence and durability of its component materials, significantly affect the need for later conservation treatment. For example, if a book printed on poor quality paper is rarely used, the paper may deteriorate faster than the binding and "repair" may never be necessary. However, if a publisher's binding for a new book is inadequate, repair may be needed after just one circulation.

The conditions under which library materials are stored also affect the need for conservation treatment. Overly warm storage conditions hasten chemical reactions and promote the aging or deterioration of all types of organic materials, including paper, bookcloth, and leather. Humid conditions stimulate the growth of mold and hasten acid deterioration, while very low humidity leads to desiccation and embrittlement. Ultraviolet rays in sunlight and fluorescent light weaken and degrade cellulosic materials, such as paper and cloth, and cause leather bindings to dry and crack. The exposure of library materials to dirt and dust causes abrasion and soiling. Air pollutants, such as sulfur dioxide and ozone, found in libraries in urban/industrial areas promote deterioration.

The way in which library materials are shelved and used also has a significant impact on the need for physical treatment or repair. Jumbled or untidy shelves, rough handling by staff and patrons, and the use of book "drops" all damage bindings and needlessly waste resources. On the other hand, proper storage and handling significantly reduce the need for conservation treatment.

Even if library materials are made sturdily, stored under optimum conditions, shelved properly, and handled carefully, a certain amount of wear and tear is inevitable with use. However, by the application of sound conservation treatments, libraries can maintain materials so that they will be available for use as long as they are needed. Of course, all organic materials are in a constant, albeit slow, state of deterioration, and *long-term* preservation requires more than simple remedial treatments. Proper repair, maintenance, and protection, however, will significantly slow down this inevitable process.

The physical maintenance, or conservation, of library materials has implications for every facet of library work. Conservation is not exclusively the concern of technical services personnel. The physical condition of an item affects its availability, and an item that is allowed to deteriorate can be completely lost to users. In many libraries, "conservation activities"—binding preparation, repair, mending, reshelving, shelf preparation, identification of damaged items — take place in more than one department. Unfortunately, in a library without an active conservation program, these activities can work against the preservation of the collections. Inadvertently, many libraries encourage the premature deterioration of their collections by simply being unaware of proper conservation practices.

Subject specialists, bibliographers, and departmental/subject divisional librarians are directly responsible for the intellectual composition of the collection. These staff members are in the best position to know an item's intrinsic value, its value to the collection as a whole, and its expected use. Unfortunately these professionals are often unaware of conservation options that can protect materials and prolong their use. Yet the conservation treatment of the collection should be their direct concern since physical access is as critical to patron satisfaction as bibliographic access.

Curators of special collections and rare book departments are often more aware of conservation because of the nature of their collections; their emphasis is on protection through limited access. Because the artifactual and monetary value of their collections can be lessened through deterioration or inappropriate treatment, these curators are necessarily aware of the need for proper conservation practices and often provide the impetus for increased conservation awareness among the entire library staff. However, often the emphasis on conservation does not extend beyond "rare" books, even though irreplaceable items and materials of permanent research value are found on the open shelves of most libraries.

Conservation treatment is but one aspect of preservation and, ultimately, the library administration is responsible for the development of a comprehensive preservation program. Although an inadequate library building may be inherited with the job and many inappropriate and damaging "policies" may be just accidents of history, an informed administrator will be aware of the impact such conditions and practices have on the preservation of the collection and take action to improve the situation by assigning preservation responsibility and authorizing the development of a preservation program. A comprehensive preservation program includes environmental control, disaster preparedness, staff and patron education, contract services for binding and preservation microfilming, reselection and replacement policies and procedures for severely deteriorated materials, handling and use policies, *as well as* in-house conservation treatment. Ideally, these separate elements are integrated into a well-organized overall program under the direction of a preservation manager. In smaller libraries, where the responsibility for aspects of a preservation program is dispersed, a preservation committee can serve a coordinating role.

For the purpose of this manual, conservation treatment includes those aspects of in-house physical maintenance and repair that prevent needless deterioration and return damaged items to usable condition. It is vitally important to link in-house conservation treatment with all aspects of an overall preservation program. In particular, contract binding (commercial library binding), replacement programs for brittle materials, and contractual arrangements for sophisticated conservation treatment should be carefully coordinated with in-house conservation activities.

In libraries where preservation needs have not been examined librarywide, the responsibility for book repair, collection preparation, and stack maintenance has typically been determined by chance and is found in several departments. Often a serials department has a book repair unit tacked onto it because binding preparation takes place there. On the other hand circulation services or departmental libraries may mend books because damaged items are found during reshelving. Cataloging departments are frequently responsible for collection preparation and may tip-in pages or "add a little tape here and there."

Regardless of its alliance with a department, book repair/mending units are usually staffed by paraprofessionals who may have no opportunity for continuing education. And they may be supervised by a professional librarian who does not have any knowledge of conservation practices. These staff members are called upon to deliver "conservation treatment" to a wide variety of library materials. They are often given instructions as precise as "patch it up" or "can't you mend it or something?" On the other hand, an informed supervisor who realizes that conservation means more than mending may be hard-pressed to effect change. Even when armed with written, tested procedures to substitute for the old methods, it is a ticklish matter to inform loyal employees that what they have been doing for years is no longer acceptable. Resistance to change, even among younger employees, can be formidable. However, the principle of benign neglect is applicable to mending and repair; if a library cannot do what is right for the materials, then it is *much better* to do nothing. Not only do inappropriate repairs waste time and money, but they usually result in irreparable damage. A positive environment for change can be created, however, when the development of a librarywide preservation program is sanctioned by the library administration and when the base of support for change is broadened through staff awareness and continuing education programs and opportunities.

This manual was developed to provide guidance for the professional librarian who manages or supervises book repair and maintenance activities as well as the paraprofessional or technician who actually does the work. As training opportunities increase, this manual ideally will be used to supplement hands-on training with an experienced conservator. The procedures in this book adhere to the best that is known about conservationally sound practices, but because each item in need of treatment presents a unique problem, none of the procedures should be performed inadvisedly. In other words, a treatment *decision* for some items should rest with the individual best equipped to determine the bibliographic and historic value of that item; it is imperative that this person be well informed of treatment options as well. Trained and experienced paraprofessionals can make excellent decisions for routine repair and maintenance providing they have access to professionals for advice in bibliographic matters, collection development, and budgeting.

To simplify the task of learning, all of the procedures in this manual are written in the same format. First the procedure is explained in general terms by listing the problem, its probable cause, and the treatment. That explanation is followed by an estimate of the time and cost for each procedure, as well as a list of the equipment and supplies needed. The procedure is then described in a step-by-step fashion for a typical item. Lastly, exceptions or special instructions are noted.

Because it is nearly impossible to fully describe with words how to do something manually, each procedure in the text is accompanied by photographs. Unfortunately, even meticulous photography could not clarify every detail and movement. A person learning a procedure will probably proceed very slowly until he/she is comfortable with manipulating the materials. Likewise, an experienced technician will soon discover a quicker way to do a procedure—either by combining steps or by possessing manual expertise not expected in the novice.

A novice learning a procedure should first read through the entire procedure and examine the photographs carefully. The necessary tools and supplies should be organized and samples for treatment chosen.

It is advisable to concentrate on learning the procedures in order. One's effort should not immediately be directed toward finding a procedure that is appropriate for some problem in hand. Later, after expertise has been developed and the procedure is familiar, the decision-making process will logically fit items to procedures. The procedures are intended to build upon each other. Specific operations included in detail in an earlier procedure are not shown in detail again.

The sequence of written steps is determined by what is most time-efficient for similar items. However, for visual continuity, the photographs may follow a slightly different order.

UNDERSTANDING TREATMENT OPTIONS

Book Repair

The seven **book**[1] repair procedures described in this manual address the major repair problems of modern **hardbound publisher's bindings**. The book repair procedures are *not* intended for the treatment of rare or unique materials. The **conservation** of rare materials requires a different approach than the **repair** of circulating books, serials, and reference works. Because rare books are usually segregated and their use restricted and supervised, their protection and long-term **preservation** is of more concern than their repair or **rebinding**. In fact, the physical condition of a rare book is part of its story, and any tampering that disrupts its bibliographic or historic evidence is not only strongly discouraged by scholars, but will lessen the value of an item.[2]

Case-bound publisher's bindings constitute the largest portion of library collections. Their disrepair is the most common conservation problem facing libraries. Despite the common nature of the problem, many libraries have not developed routine procedures for book repair and **preventative maintenance**. This failing may be a librarian's simple aversion to the "housekeeper" image. Also, *building* a collection interests most librarians more than maintaining it.

Wear and tear on library books is not only inevitable, it is philosophically desirable since it is a definite indication that books are being *used*. Unfortunately, disrepair is not exclusively caused by ordinary use; it also results from inadequate or poorly executed publisher's bindings, improper shelving and book return practices, or damaging storage environments. Regardless of the source of disrepair, a simple repair executed in time may eliminate the need later for expensive, time-consuming repair or rebinding.

At a commercial edition bindery, the **case (cover)** and the **text block** of a case bound book are made in separate production lines and glued together in a final step termed **"casing-in."** The **attachment** of the case to the text block is critical to its purpose of protecting the contents. This attachment can break down for a number of reasons. For example, the casing-in step may not have been done correctly by the binder. The chemistry of adhesives and the complexity of production machinery add up to a myriad of potential problems. It is not uncommon for a new book either to arrive loose in its case or to loosen almost immediately.

Case-bound books are meant to stand upright on their tails. A book that is placed on its **fore-edges** (either while awaiting reshelving or for lack of space) will eventually pull out of its cover. The **hinges** cannot support the full weight of the book when it is on its fore-edges and the shape of the **spine** will soon become concave instead of convex.

Book returns that allow books to drop *any* distance or to jostle roughly against each other are extremely destructive; the book's physical structure is simply *not* designed to withstand the shock. In addition to broken corners and torn pages, dropping a book causes the heavier contents to yank away from the cover. This is sometimes so dramatic that a book literally tears out of its cover.

A book that is loose in its case is the most common library **maintenance** problem. Every circulating collection would benefit from a regular program of stack inspection to locate books that are loose in their cases—especially in heavily used portions of the collection. Staff members and part-time assistants can be easily trained to recognize

---

[1]Each term defined in the glossary of this book is printed in boldface the first time it appears in the text.
[2]For additional readings concerning this issue, see items 5, 18, 31, and 42 of the Selected Bibliography.

this problem. If books are caught at the point where they are merely loose, the repair is inexpensive because the hinges can be tightened by the simple application of glue.[3]

Once a text block has become loose in its case the vulnerable **hinge area** is stressed and the result is often a torn **endsheet**. This problem can be easily repaired by replacing the damaged endsheet after tightening the hinges. If the text block is allowed to remain loose, it will eventually tear away from the cover, and the book will require **recasing** or rebinding.

Even when a book is cased-in and shelved properly, its spine and hinge areas inevitably wear out first. The hinge is flexed during opening. Both the **head** of the book and its spine are yanked when it is taken off the shelf and jammed when it is returned to the shelf. Ultraviolet rays in sunlight or fluorescent light weaken and degrade the exposed spine of a shelved book. Therefore, the phenomenon of the "backs coming off" is common to all library collections.

If the spine lettering is still legible, a simple repair can replace the **deteriorated** spine with a new **bookcloth** spine. The original spine, with its frayed edges neatly trimmed, is **mounted** onto a new spine. This repair is cheaper than having the book recased at a **library bindery** and does not disrupt the sewing. Since the original **cover boards** are retained and the original spine mounted, the book has much the same appearance and re**titling** and remarking are unnecessary. Finally, a repair executed **in-house** reduces the length of time the book is unavailable for use. However, this repair is not sufficient when the case is excessively worn or the item is expected to receive continued heavy use.

Very few publisher's bindings are designed to withstand the rigors of library use. Additionally, as production costs rise, the first cutbacks are usually made in the quality of the bookwork: **"perfect" bindings** replace sewn **sections**; the cloth **super** is eliminated from the casing-in process; spines are **flat back** instead of **rounded and backed**; and **paperbacks** are issued instead of hardbound **editions**. Since newer books circulate more frequently than older books, it is unfortunate that libraries often receive new books in progressively weaker bindings. Even ordinary use will hasten the deterioration of already inadequate bindings. Thick, heavy, and oversize books are especially subject to damage because frequently their bindings are not correspondingly stronger.

Libraries cannot afford to have every book they acquire with an inadequate publisher's binding rebound by a commercial library bindery. The result, in any event, would be very boring. Although a **library binding** for a book in disrepair would probably outlast the book itself and thus solve the problem once and for all, it would be an unnecessary expense for many items. Based on projected future use, a simple repair may be all the maintenance needed, particularly as the date of publication becomes less current and the book circulates less frequently.

A case-bound book is typically held into its cover by super (cloth) and endsheets (sheets of heavy paper folded in half). The super is glued to the spine of the text block and extends as a hinge onto the cover boards. The folded edge of the endsheets is **tipped onto** the front and back of the text block, and half the sheet is glued to the inside of the cover boards during casing-in. If done correctly, this method of attachment, although not as secure as attachment by **cords** or **tapes**[4], suffices for most books. Unfortunately, the super used in most publisher's bindings resembles weak cheesecloth. Even worse for libraries (since super is unseen by the buyer), more and more hardbound publisher's bindings do not include super at all! Obviously, endsheets tipped 3 mm onto a text block will not support its attachment to a cover for long.

---

[3]This technique was first published by conservator Carolyn Horton. See item 16 of the Selected Bibliography.

[4]Traditional hand bookbinding involved sewing each section in turn around cords or tapes and locking the sewing at the head and tail. The cords or tapes were then laced into the cover boards or glued to them. In 1882, the **Smyth sewing** machine was invented, enabling sections to be sewn together on a continuous thread and through-the-fold **sewing over tapes** or cords was gradually dropped altogether.

The characteristic curved shape of a book's spine is formed during a step called "rounding and backing." Besides contributing to **openability**, the convex shape helps keep a book from sagging forward away from its cover. Unfortunately, many modern books are not rounded at all (flat back), or they are improperly rounded, or their shape is inadequately supported by glue and spine **linings**.

The critical attachment between the text block and cover of a modern binding often breaks down long before the cover is worn out and sometimes before the book is even used.[5] If the cover is in good condition, weak original components can be replaced with sound materials, and the book can be recased. This solution is desirable in terms of time and money when both the cover and the text block are intact, although detached from each other.

Recasing also can be a solution for books detached and deteriorated because of normal wear and tear. Torn endsheets and super are often accompanied by a cover that is torn or deteriorated in the hinge area. If appropriate to the title and its projected use, the spine area can be reinforced with new bookcloth and the book recased.

Because the hinge area of a book is the most vulnerable area, it is not uncommon for the first or last sections of a sewn text block to have loosened or detached. Loose sections must be reattached before further repairs can be performed.

Informed use of library bindery services is essential to the maintenance of circulating collections. Having an original cover replaced by a library binder is recommended when an item needs a new cover because it has received heavy use (such as a reference work) or is circulated frequently (such as a textbook or novel). However, in addition to full rebinding, most library binders provide "new case" (recasing) services for customers. Recasing, as opposed to rebinding, replaces only the cover, endsheets, and spine linings. Sections and original sewing are retained, and the book is not trimmed. The method of endsheet attachment, however, is an important consideration; when possible, new endsheets should be sewn on through-the-fold.

For the older, retrospective work whose binding has deteriorated with age or from abuse prior to its being added to the library, or for materials that have very weak paper, it may be advisable to recase the item in-house—provided the original binding has no **historic value**. Constructing a new cover in-house is not as hard on the item physically. Also, there may be more choices available in terms of binding style, **structure**, and the materials used than the library's contract binder can provide. Many items needing a new cover are simply too fragile to withstand the rigors of the bindery production line.

Maintenance

In addition to routine book repair activities, libraries have other conservation challenges. The five maintenance procedures included in this manual suggest solutions to some common problems.

Items such as unbound paperbacks and **pamphlets** must be bound or protected prior to being made available for use. The majority of these items can be bound by a library bindery. However, in some instances, in-house treatment is preferable. For example, many items received as paperbacks in a library are **single-section** pamphlets. Their pages are folded in the center and stapled, usually to a heavier-weight paper cover. Because of the ephemeral nature of most of this material and its brevity, pamphlets are particularly suitable for simple in-house binding. Music scores issued in a

---

[5]Returning an unused, damaged volume to the publisher for replacement will not solve the problem since inadequate binding will be uniform for the edition.

single-section **format** with accompanying parts are also suitable for in-house pamphlet binding.

While an in-house binding is inexpensive in time and materials, a library binding for a pamphlet costs as much, or more, than a binding for an ordinary book. The commercial binding will be constructed of **bookboard** covered with a **synthetic** bookcloth, and although **durable**, it is perhaps more binding than needed and often no more desirable from a conservation standpoint than an in-house product. In addition, not all paperbacks acquired by a library are suitable for mass-production paperback binding by a library bindery. An item may be unacceptable in the paperback production line if it is less than 1.5 cm thick, if its **inner margins** are too narrow for even the slightest trimming, or if it contains folded pages. Likewise, the paper in older paperbacks may be too fragile to be bound by machine.[6] Paperbacks with text blocks composed of folded sections sewn through-the-fold should be given a case binding at the library bindery so that the sewn format can be retained. These items must be examined carefully because at first glance, **burst bindings**, a form of **adhesive binding**, resemble sewn sections.

The most common problem paperback is one with **coated paper**. Paper that is coated, especially thick paper, is unsuitable for adhesive binding because the slick paper never adheres properly to glue, and the pages inevitably fall out. This process is greatly accelerated if the **grain direction** of the paper runs crosswise to the spine (the book is printed cross grain) because the stress on the adhesive binding is greatly increased. Many exhibition catalogs and photography and art books are issued on coated stock and given a paper cover. Frequently these items have **machine-sewn sections**. If the sections are trimmed and the items adhesive bound at a library bindery, they become a permanent problem on the shelves. Library binders are experimenting with new adhesive binding methods that promise a more durable product. Some can combine **notching** of pages with adhesive binding and produce excellent results. Adhesive binding services should be discussed with the library's contract binder and examples examined and tested.

Many items acquired by libraries are used infrequently or superseded. In addition to materials that may be unsuitable for commercial library binding because of coated paper, narrow inner margins, or an unusual format, these items may also be candidates for a simple in-house binding.

The simplest in-house maintenance procedure for paperbacks attaches **cambric** hinges to the inside **joints** and **reinforcing** boards of **bristol** to the inside covers. This binding does not improve the strength of the original page attachment method, but is suitable for infrequently used items, items that will be superseded, or items that are needed immediately. For more heavily used items, a library may choose to reinforce the covers by attaching protective cover boards and a **buckram** spine piece to the paperback. Again, the original page attachment method is not affected.

Staff who are sorting paperbacks for binding must have a clear understanding of *all* the available binding options, or their library will accrue future conservation and maintenance problems.

In the past, **mending** tears and voids in paper documents (such as book pages, maps, prints, or manuscripts) has been the only in-house "conservation" activity assiduously practiced by libraries. Unfortunately, due to lack of information, libraries have almost universally mended tears with some type of **pressure-sensitive tape**. In addition, book bindings have not escaped the horrors of the tape dispenser. Most collections contain examples of the liberal application of everything from "book tape"

---

[6]Some binders use **cleat sewing** for paperbacks. Since cleat sewing intrudes on the inner margin and produces a rigid, flat spine, it is an unacceptable method of binding for paperbacks, or for that matter, anything but the most ephemeral materials.

to cellophane, surgical, or electrician's tape. Tape is convenient to use, but cannot be recommended except for the most ephemeral materials.[7] Within a short time, the adhesive on the tape deteriorates, leaving a sticky residue, and staining and embrittling the paper. Tape removal from rare materials is a time consuming process that must be performed by a professional conservator. Frequently the stains and damage remain even after the tape and adhesive have been removed with solvents.

Conservators use many different techniques for mending tears and voids, including applying **paper pulp** with a **leaf-casing** machine and an elaborate method that uses matching paper beveled and joined to the original. However, for overall ease of application and proven safeness, a technique using a **water-torn** strip of **Japanese paper** applied to the tear with **starch paste** is highly recommended. When applied carefully, the mend is unobtrusive, **reversible**, and permanent. Application under the direction of a conservator or informed curator is even suitable for rare/unique materials.

Coated paper, however, should not be mended using starch paste because of the effect of water on the coating. Instead, tears on coated paper should be mended using heat-set tissue made to the specifications of the Library of Congress Preservation Office or another well-known conservation laboratory. This tissue is available commercially.

Most library collections contain large numbers of **leather-bound** books that present a discouraging maintenance problem. *Simple* book repair techniques are not possible for leather bindings, and the typical commercial library binding is not suitable for most 18th and 19th century items. Yet leather books of this period were not bound as sturdily as previous centuries and are frequently in a state of serious disrepair. As bookbinding became a lay trade and the demand for books increased, shortcuts in craftsmanship appeared. In most cases, changes made for the sake of economy and speed sacrificed the functional qualities of the binding.

Although leather is an extremely durable **covering material** for books, dirt, overly dry and hot storage conditions, or humid conditions that promote fungal growth can seriously reduce its flexibility and strength. Additionally, vegetable-tanned leather manufactured since the eighteenth century is subject to **acid deterioration**, either from acid left from the tanning process, or from the absorption of sulfur dioxide (which changes to sulfuric acid) in polluted urban and industrial environments. Protective buffering salts present in earlier leather bindings are missing from most leather produced after 1700. Without a buffer against acid attack, leather suffers from chemical deterioration, which in its extreme is a weak, powdery condition termed "red rot."[8]

Traditionally, the treatment of leather bindings has been largely a matter of established practice and personal preference based on experience. Unfortunately, there is no conclusive evidence that any one treatment process under a given circumstance is best for the treatment of leather. In fact, research to date indicates that little benefit accrues from *any* of the treatments currently practiced! The best protection for a leather binding seems to be proper environmental conditions and custom-made **protective enclosures**. Because not enough is known about the long-term effects of leather treatment, most conservators advise against treating leather bindings beyond removing surface dirt with a dust cloth such as One Wipe®; placing interleaving sheets between the cover boards and the text block to prevent **acid migration** from the leather **turn-ins**; and providing a protective enclosure.

---

[7]Only one tape—Archival Aids®—has been recommended by some conservators as safe to use for materials that will not be kept in the permanent collections of libraries.

[8]For further information see item 13 of the Selected Bibliography.

Protective Enclosure

Protective enclosure is chosen as a conservation option when actual physical treatment is inadvisable or not possible for the moment. Treatment may be inadvisable in view of an item's condition or expected use, or because treatment would adversely affect the **bibliographic integrity** or monetary value of an item. Enclosures may also be provided simply as physical protection for valuable, damaged, or vulnerable materials; as a first step or **phased conservation** for an item or group of items that will eventually receive full conservation treatment; or as a supplement to **full conservation treatment**.

The purpose of any type of protective enclosure[9] is to protect an item from **mechanical damage** and, in varying degrees, to mitigate the effects of environmental agents of deterioration such as dirt, air pollution, and light. This protection can range from an elaborate airtight temperature and humidity-controlled exhibit case to a simple wrapper made from **alkaline** materials. The five protective enclosure procedures included in this manual illustrate a range of enclosures that meet most conservation needs.

Encapsulation, the technique of enclosing fragile, **brittle**, vulnerable, or damaged flat paper documents in a polyester film envelope, was developed as an alternative to cellulose acetate lamination, which was devised by William J. Barrow in 1935. As practiced today, lamination involves sealing a **deacidified** document between sheets of tissue and film. By the application of intense heat (340-360 degrees Farenheit) and pressure, the laminates impregnate the fibers of the paper and therefore reinforce a weak document.

Both lamination and encapsulation provide physical support or strength to an item, but encapsulation has a number of advantages over lamination. First, encapsulation is instantly and completely reversible, unlike lamination. Secondly, the technique of encapsulation is easily learned and requires only inexpensive equipment, whereas the cost of a laminating machine may be prohibitively high except for large conservation facilities. Thirdly, the intense heat and pressure exerted on a document during lamination, and the difficulty of obtaining a reliable cellulose acetate film, make lamination a risky business for archival documents (items that will be kept in a collection indefinitely).[10]

The polyester film used in encapsulation is a stable, inert substance that is very strong, dimensionally stable, and widely available in a range of thicknesses and sizes. The Preservation Research and Testing Office at the Library of Congress has tested polyester film and found it appropriate for conservation purposes. The technique of encapsulation involves sandwiching a document between two sheets of polyester film. The sandwich is either held together with double-sided tape, ultrasonics, or heat sealed at the edges. Because of the static charge created by the film, encapsulation cannot be used for items with images made in pencil or charcoal (pastels).

It should be kept in mind that a *chemically unstable* document deteriorating as a result of high acid content receives no benefits from encapsulation other than the considerable benefit of *physical protection*. It is preferable if items needing **neutralization and alkaline buffering** are treated prior to encapsulation. De-acidification can only be performed safely, however, with adequate facilities and under the supervision of a conservator. If a chemically unstable document is also fragile or damaged, it is perfectly acceptable to encapsulate it, providing it is understood that the item should be deacidified when feasible. When possible, a sheet of alkaline paper should be encapsulated with an acidic item; this technique will alleviate

---

[9]I.e., portfolio, box, folder, wrapper, microenvironment, etc.

[10]See item 24 of the Selected Bibliography.

the increased rate of deterioration caused by trapping an acidic item in a relatively airtight envelope.[11]

Polyester film encapsulation is also a suitable technique for protecting items from physical wear and tear caused by frequent use. A folder made of polyester film sealed on two edges can temporarily be used to protect fragile items that are being examined by a patron. Likewise, a sheet of film can be laid over a large document or map to protect it during use.

A **portfolio** or box protects a book by providing a **microenvironment** — a buffer against rapid fluctuations in temperature and humidity, and protection from dust, light, atmospheric pollutants, and mechanical damage. To be effective, the enclosure must be custom-made from permanent and durable materials to fit the item *exactly* and allow for easy removal and replacement of the book by users. The typical "slip case" may serve as a decorative accompaniment to a rare book or limited edition, but does not provide proper protection from a conservation point of view.

The type of portfolio or box chosen to protect a particular item should be appropriate for the item's format, size and weight, value, and projected use. Simple portfolios constructed to protect seldom-used materials for which binding is inappropriate or unfeasible can often be made from "scraps" that are left over from other procedures. A lightweight portfolio, however, is only suitable for lightweight items. Heavier items, or items that warrant a more durable enclosure because of expected use, can be protected by a "phase box," or four-flap portfolio, made from heavy-duty **boxboard**. The phase box illustrated in this manual is a modified version of the phase box designed by conservators at the Library of Congress.[12]

A custom-made, cloth-covered "double tray box"[13] constructed from heavy-duty binder's board or alkaline **matboard** has long been a standard conservation treatment for rare books. Providing a protective box for a book can be an alternative to rebinding or time-consuming repair. Physical treatment can disrupt or obscure important bibliographic, historic, or artificial evidence of a binding contemporary with the period of the book's production. In addition, when full conservation treatment has been provided, a protective enclosure is a logical addendum. Protective enclosure is also chosen when specific treatments for a particular item are questionable and better methods may be developed in the future with improved technology and continued research.

Most frequently, however, enclosure is chosen because libraries simply do not have the resources to do all the conservation treatment needed to stabilize the *physical condition* of a damaged item. Enclosure can be a holding measure that protects items from further mechanical damage while awaiting treatment in the future. On the other hand, even if there were enough time and money to treat every book that needed it, that would not always be the best decision in terms of the collection or the individual items. Enclosure can be an option when rebinding or conservation treatment cannot be justified in terms of a damaged book's expected use or **intrinsic value**.

As a conservation measure, enclosure is highly recommended for retrospective materials because it provides maximum physical protection from environmental hazards with a minimum expenditure of time, skills, and materials.

Protective enclosure in a portfolio or box will not solve the problem of a book with brittle paper that is needed for use. Enclosure can be a holding measure, but further treatment will be needed if a brittle item is to be returned to usable condition.

---

[11]See item 39 of the Selected Bibliography.

[12]For a more in depth discussion of LC's phased conservation program, see item 3 of the Selected Bibliography.

[13]Also called Solander box, drop-spine box, clam-shell box, three-piece folding box, rare book box, etc. The Solander box named after David Solander (d.1782), a Swedish botanist working at the British Museum, was actually a leather-covered wooden case intended for the protection of botanical specimens.

Preservation microfilming is the technique typically chosen to preserve the *information* contained in books with brittle paper. However, there are many instances when preservation of the original text pages is preferred. A title may contain illustrations, especially in color, that are not adequately reproduced by microfilming. And, items such as atlases may be more useful to the library patron when preserved in their original format. In addition, some items have artifactual or intrinsic value that should dictate retention of the original.

One practical technique for preserving original, brittle pages in a book involves separating the text into individual leaves, neutralizing and alkaline buffering the paper, encapsulating each leaf in polyester film, binding the leaves together, and providing a hard cover. Although time-consuming, the construction of a polyester book is a preservation alternative to microfilming materials that should be kept in their original format. However, a polyester book will obviously not resemble the original and may not be a satisfactory alternative for an item whose binding is of historic interest. In this case, retention of the binding **fragments** (such as decorated cover boards) combined with **photodocumentation** of the original, may adequately preserve important information about the original binding.

ORGANIZING AND SUPERVISING THE CONSERVATION WORKSHOP

Priorities and Decision Making

Before a hand is lifted in treatment, a library should first determine conservation priorities based on the nature of the collection and how it is used. For example, a college library whose collection is heavily used by undergraduate students should probably concentrate on simple book repair for current material, while a historical society library might emphasize the protective enclosure of manuscripts and rare books.[14]

To a library embarking on an expanded conservation program, the amount of work to be done may seem overwhelming. Therefore, priorities should start with those activities that will have the most significant and immediate impact on the condition of the collection as a whole. For example, with the goal of preventative maintenance in mind, a library might survey their collection and concentrate on simple book repairs before embarking on more complicated and time-consuming conservation procedures. Priorities should be periodically reevaluated as the overall maintenance of a collection is enhanced. For example, a library that first concentrated on routine book repair for heavily used collections might follow with a systematic program of protective enclosure for older, retrospective materials of permanent research value.

Once priorities are determined, a library should standardize criteria for treatment decision making. This does not mean that every item in a similar state of disrepair will receive the same treatment, but rather that treatment decisions will be based on a standard method of evaluation. A treatment decision is based on the current and projected condition of an item, its intrinsic value, and its current and projected use.[15] However, each library should determine its own specific criteria based on the nature of the collection. For example, it is logical that the same damaged book about native Americans published in 1874 could receive different treatment at two different

---

[14]See appendix 2, "Developing In-House Capabilities: Profiles of Four Hypothetical Libraries," for an example of matching priorities to the needs of a particular collection.

[15]See appendix 1, "Decision-Making Checklist for Book Repair," for an example of a decision-making strategy.

libraries. Library 1, a research library with a strong ethnographic collection supporting graduate programs, might expect frequent use and spend considerable time on conservation treatment for the book. Library 2 at a four-year college might simply provide an inexpensive portfolio.

Decision making is also affected by the priorities set for a collection. For example, if eliminating the backlog of books needing repair is a priority, items that *could* be inexpensively recased in-house in their original covers might instead by sent to a commercial library bindery for recasing. Then conservation staff would be free to concentrate on repairing the bulk of items needing very simple repair. Once the backlog was eliminated, more time-consuming repairs could be added to in-house production.

Treatment decision making must also take into account the options that are available to a particular library and the cost of treatment. "Doing nothing" is a viable option for items whose treatment is beyond the expertise of local personnel, or items whose value does not warrant the cost of treatment.

Not only do many libraries face backlogs of items in need of treatment, they may also be limited in the resources they are able to allocate to reduce those backlogs. However, *if the need for and benefits of conservation action is recognized,* funds and staff for an adequate conservation effort can usually be found within the budget of a library by making organizational changes and streamlining inefficient activities. Consolidating all those activities that affect the **physical item** increases the efficiency of operations and saves time and money. *Direct* savings can be realized if improved maintenance reduces the amount of rebinding or replacement necessary.

Making treatment decisions can commence once priorities are established and a rationale for treatment decision making determined. The novice might benefit from listing available options and evaluating each item based on the list.[16] Making decisions about treatment is like taking an exam: the best strategy is to make the easy decisions first and come back to the hard ones. Often further exploration of an item is necessary, such as finding out about additional copies, the condition of a volume set, or consulting with staff or faculty concerning use. Such explorations will often make a decision obvious.

Training and Productivity

Conserving library materials is a task vast enough to require streamlining procedures as well as the application, where appropriate, of the principles of mass production. Devising standard treatment procedures to address the common conservation problems facing libraries will increase productivity and enhance the quality of the work. Once treatment procedures are developed and a decision-making routine established, productivity will depend on a well-trained staff with positive attitudes, wise management of personnel and material resources, and a *well-organized workshop.*

A library already engaged in "mending" activities usually faces its greatest challenge in developing in-house capabilities for performing even simple conservationally sound treatments. Change is often viewed as threatening by staff who are accustomed to doing things the old way. However, the well-being of a collection *cannot* be compromised by permitting damaging practices to continue.

Without the total cooperation of all staff assigned to conservation, a productive atmosphere is not possible. Thus, it is often better in the long run to transfer uncooperative staff to another library unit and replace them with staff who have a

---

[16]For a good example of this technique, see item 8 of the Selected Bibliography.

genuine interest in conservation. Supervisors and managers must be alert to staff who pretend to accept change but who actually will obstruct progress at every opportunity.

The best approach to training staff to perform simple conservation treatments is demonstration combined with observation and feedback. A supervisor should first discuss the context in which a treatment is applied. That is, how did the item reach a state of disrepair or deterioration, what can be done to correct it or to protect the item from further deterioration or damage, and what treatment decision was made and why. It is not enough to simply tell trainees what to do; an understanding of *why* they are doing it is critical to remembering *what* to do, as well as to developing an appreciation for the value of the work. A new employee should be encouraged to ask questions and discuss the issues involved.

The second step should be a demonstration of the procedure on a typical item from start to finish. Each step should be explained in detail. Thirdly, the trainee should perform the procedure step-by-step for an individual item with constant direction from the supervisor. Fourth, the trainee should perform the procedure on a "batch" of three to five typical items. Batch production, which involves performing the same step for several items before going on to the next step, is more efficient than item-by-item production. The supervisor should observe technique, guiding the trainee where he varies from the standard procedure. The efficiency of following the established order of the steps should be emphasized. Fifth, the trainee should be left alone to work on another batch and the completed items checked carefully for problems. From the start, an unacceptable product should be frankly discussed; it is both unwise and unfair to assume that a person will eventually "catch on" by themselves.

Finally, during the training period (which will vary depending on the person and the procedure), the trainee should be observed often and the quality and quantity of his work discussed. Mistakes are expected in the beginning and trainees should be advised not to be ashamed of or reticent about them. A substantial investment of time taken to train a new employee is *definitely* worth it. Not only do people naturally respond to attention, but if training is taken seriously, the employee is likely to develop a serious attitude towards the work.

An employee should be taught one procedure at a time, left to it long enough to master it thoroughly, and then taught a more difficult procedure. Periodic observation and evaluation of the employee's technique by the supervisor will help to avoid problems and increase productivity. However, not everyone is suited for conservation work; if retraining is continually necessary, it is usually best to transfer the person or terminate employment.[17] Poor performance is sometimes just the result of boredom. To avoid the problem of a competent but bored employee, the work should be varied as much as possible and responsibilities proportionally increased with abilities. Praise of quality work and reward through interesting and challenging assignments are never a mistake.

After a reasonable time period, the new employee's productivity on a particular procedure should be determined based on at least one week's output. From the beginning, an employee should understand that he will be expected to *produce*. The productivity of a particular individual can be objectively measured by determining an average time for each procedure and checking output against hours spent working, minus breaks and clean-up time.

Standards for productivity are beneficial for both management and employees. Initially, there can be considerable apprehension, but employee involvement in "trials" to determine a standard rate for a particular procedure will encourage acceptance. Making employees aware of how much they produce will have a *dramatic* effect on overall workshop productivity. Also, a measurement of productivity will provide a

---

[17]See appendix 4, "Dexterity Test," for a method of evaluating the potential of applicants for conservation work.

supervisor with a management tool for determining how much can be accomplished within a certain time frame and for estimating the quantity of supplies needed.

Employees can not be expected to work efficiently unless the workshop itself is well organized and maintained. Work "stations" can be organized so that all the equipment, tools, and supplies necessary for routine treatment are on hand or conveniently located.[18] It is a good idea to appoint a shop "foreman" to replenish supplies and keep the workshop organized. Certain rules are always necessary to maintain order, such as proper cleaning of tools, use of equipment, and organization of work-in-progress. When an employee arrives each day to a clean, spacious, well-equipped work area he is naturally encouraged to produce. Additionally, the workshop "atmosphere" is important; the morale of the workers, their teamwork or lack of it, peer group pressure, and the sociability of the group—all these elements will affect the productivity of the workshop.

---

[18]See pages 204 and 205 for photographs of a book repair work station and supplies station.

2
Book Repair Procedures

TIGHTENING THE HINGES OF A CASE-BOUND BOOK

Problem
- Text block sagging or pulling away from its cover.

Causes
- Inadequate publisher's binding, especially poor **adhesion** in the hinge area.
- Damaging book return systems.
- Improper shelving practices, especially fore-edge shelving and leaning books.
- Rough handling or dropping.
- Inadequate rounding and backing or a flat-back spine, especially on a heavy book.
- Normal wear and tear from frequent use.

Treatment
- Tighten the attachment of the text block to its cover by applying glue into the hinge area.

Cost
- Batch production at approximately 5 minutes per item.
- Materials cost per item negligible.

Equipment and Supplies
- Book press
- Metal-edged pressing boards
- Knitting needles, metal (two sizes)
- Bone folder
- Glue brush
- Artist's oil painting brush (long, narrow brush with short bristles)
- **Polyvinyl acetate (PVA) adhesive** (dilute 5:1, PVA:water)
- Waxed paper
- Empty dish-detergent bottle (or other narrow container approximately 25 cm tall)

Operating Procedures—Typical Sequence
1. Select for repair when the book is loose in the hinge area, but its super and endsheets are still intact (photo 1).
2. Place the book on its tail with the cover open. When the hinges are loose, the text block can be pressed away from the cover, exposing the inside of the hinges (photo 2).
3. Dip a knitting needle of appropriate size into a tall, narrow bottle filled with slightly diluted PVA. The needle should be coated completely with glue.
4. Carefully insert the needle into the hinge area between the spine of the text block and the spine of the case, and roll the needle into the joint (photo 3). Care must be taken not to get glue on the spine, or the book will be severely stressed when opened.
5. Lay the book flat and **bone** in the hinge (photo 4). Repeat steps 3, 4, and 5 for the other hinge.
6. Open the covers and place waxed paper between the cover board and the text block to prevent any glue seeping through from damaging the paper in the inner hinge.

7. **Press** the book between metal-edged boards in a book press (photo 5). The metal lips on the boards press into the hinge areas as the book press is tightened.

Special Instructions

- A book may be only slightly loose in the hinge areas, or the super and endsheet may have lifted several inches off the cover board. In both instances, the purpose of the repair is to secure the book in its case by regluing the parts that have lifted away. This very simple repair is possible only when the endsheets and super are intact (not torn).
- If the loose area is large, a brush should be used to apply the glue.
- If a whole batch of "tightening hinges" are being done, books can be removed from the press after 15 minutes and laid flat on top of each other (staggered spine to fore-edge) until they are completely **dry**.

TIGHTENING THE HINGES OF A CASE-BOUND BOOK

Illustrated

1—Select for repair when the book is loose in the hinge area.

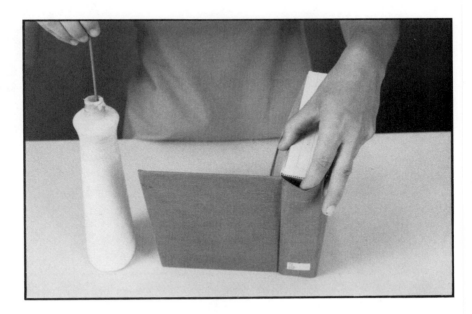

2 — Press the text block away from the cover to expose the inside of the hinges.

3 — Insert a knitting needle covered with glue into the hinge area and roll it into the joint.

4—Lay the book flat and bone in the hinge.

5—Press the book between metal-edged boards in a book press.

REPLACING A TORN ENDSHEET

Problem
- Endsheet torn in the hinge area.
- Torn or damaged **fly leaf**.

Causes
- Normal wear and tear from frequent use.
- Improper shelving practices.
- Inattention to loose hinges.
- Deliberate mutilation of a fly leaf.

Treatment
- Replace the damaged endsheet(s) with new alkaline endsheet(s). If necessary, tighten the attachment of the text block into the case.

Cost
- Batch production at approximately 7 minutes per item.
- Materials cost approximately 15 cents per item.

Equipment and Supplies
- Board shear or table top model paper cutter
- Book press or wrapped fire brick
- Metal-edged pressing boards or metal knitting needles and a thin plywood board
- Glue brush
- Bone folder
- Scalpel
- Cork-backed metal ruler
- Endsheets, alkaline, single-fold in precut sizes
- Goyu or Sekishu (Japanese paper) strips, 2 cm wide
- Polyvinyl acetate (PVA) adhesive (dilute 3:1, PVA:water)
- **Mixture** of PVA and starch paste (1:3)
- Wastepaper
- Waxed paper
- Scrap piece of board

Operating Procedures — Typical Sequence
1. Select a book for repair when its endsheet is torn in the hinge area, but its super is still intact and its cover is in reasonably good condition (photo 1).
2. Remove the original endsheet by grasping the fly leaf with the left hand, placing the right hand firmly on the text block, and easing the tipped-on fly leaf away from the first section (photo 2).
3. Peel away loose fragments of the endsheet where it is glued down over the super on the cover board. While supporting the text block, carefully open the cover so that the spine lies over the edge of the table and the hinge meets the rim. Sand the cover board lightly so the new endsheet will lie smoothly (photo 3). If necessary, repeat this process for the other endsheet.
4. Select new endsheets slightly larger than the text block (photo 4).
5. Reinforce the folds of the endsheets (optional) with a 2-cm strip of Goyu or Sekishu pasted with mixture (photos 5, 6, and 7).
6. Trim the endsheets to the exact height of the text block and tip them on (photo 8).
   a. Place the folded edge of the new endsheets between two strips of waste paper and apply glue to a 3-mm wide area along the fold (photo 9).
   b. Carefully position the endsheet on the text block and bone the folded edge against the **shoulder** (photo 10). If the endsheet is misplaced, the book will not open properly.
7. Close the cover and bone in the hinge (photo 11).
8. Trim the endsheet(s) to the exact width of the text block.
   a. Place a strip of board between the cover board and the endsheet.

b. Place a cork-backed metal ruler between the new endsheet and the text block. (The ruler should line up *exactly* with the fore-edge of the text block.)

c. Using a scalpel, remove the excess endsheet (photo 12).

9. Attach the new endsheet(s) to the cover board.

a. Open the cover and apply glue to the new endsheet with a mixture of PVA and starch paste. The brushing motion should start in the center of the page and move vertically, or with the grain direction of the paper (photo 13). Apply adhesive lightly and evenly.

b. Carefully close the cover over the glued endsheet (photo 14) and bone in the hinge.

c. While supporting the text block, open the front cover so that the spine lies over the edge of the table and the hinge meets the rim. Smooth the endsheet by rubbing with a soft cloth or boning *over* a piece of waste paper (photo 15). Do not open the cover more than 140 degrees or the endsheet will stretch, causing a crease in the joint.

10. If the corners of the cover are frayed, apply a little PVA and smooth the frayed threads in place.

11. Place waxed paper in the folds of the endsheets (photo 16) and **weight** the book until dry (photo 17).

Special Instructions

•   If a book press is not available, a book can be pressed by laying metal knitting needles into the hinges, covering the book with a thin plywood board, and weighting with a wrapped brick or other heavy object.

•   When an endsheet has begun to tear, the text block may also be loose in the case. Usually the text block is secured when the endsheets are replaced because the super is exposed to glue during the procedure. However, the text block should be carefully checked.

•   Although it may only be *necessary* to replace one endsheet, it may be *advisable* to replace both endsheets at the same time.

•   To save time and materials, endsheets should be precut in a variety of sizes or purchased precut.

•   Endsheets should be cut so that the grain direction of the paper runs *parallel* with the spine of the book. The grain direction of paper is the machine direction of the paper fibers, or the direction in which most of the fibers in a machine-made paper lie. Grain direction is determined by flexing a sheet of paper; the way the paper bends most easily is the grain direction. If in doubt, a square piece of paper when wetted on one side will curl into a tube parallel with the grain direction. If the grain direction of the text paper runs crosswise (perpendicular to the spine), a book will tend to snap shut instead of opening properly. If the grain direction of the endsheets or cover boards runs crosswise, the cover will **warp**.

REPLACING A TORN ENDSHEET

Illustrated

1 — Select for repair when an endsheet is torn or damaged, but the super is intact.

2 — Remove the old fly leaves.

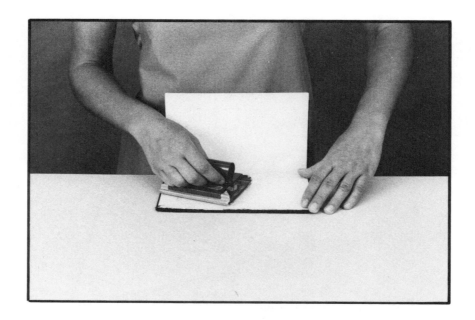

3 — Sand the cover boards.

4 — Select new endsheets slightly larger than the text block.

5 — Paste a strip of Japanese paper with mixture.

6 — Position the strip so that its center is over the fold of the endsheet.

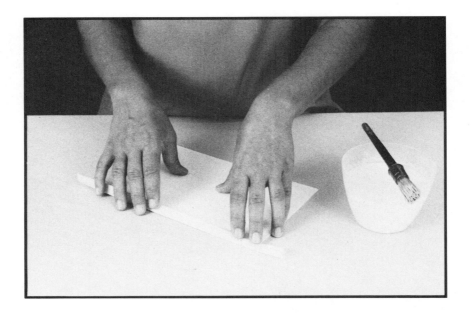

7 — Flip the endsheet, smoothing down the other half of the strip.

8 — Trim the new endsheets to the exact height of the text block.

9 — Apply glue to a strip 3 mm wide on the folded edge of the new endsheets.

10 — Bone the folded edge of the endsheet against the shoulder of the text block.

11 — Close the cover and bone in the hinge.

12 — Trim the width of the endsheet to the *exact* width of the text block.

13 — Brushing vertically from the center out, apply glue to the endsheet.

14 — Close the cover over the glued endsheet.

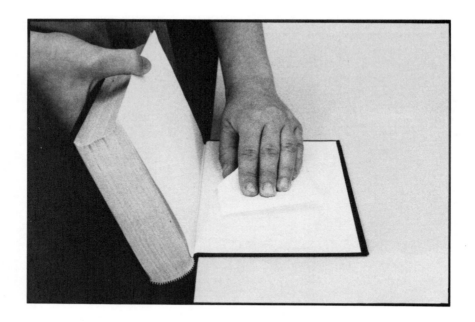

15—Smooth the endsheet while carefully supporting the text block.

16—Place waxed paper in the fold of the endsheet.

17—Weight the book until dry.

NEW BOOKCLOTH SPINE WITH MOUNTED ORIGINAL SPINE

Problem
- Torn or seriously weakened cloth in the hinge area.
- Torn or missing cloth at the head or tail.

Causes
- Normal wear and tear in the hinge area from frequent use.
- Weak original covering material.
- Rough or careless handling.
- Improper shelving practices.
- Damage to the spine from exposure to ultraviolet light in sunlight or fluorescent light.
- Wrong size or improperly made original spine.

Treatment
- Replace the damaged spine with a new spine made from matching bookcloth that has been reinforced with a tightly-woven muslin (super).
- Replace the kraft paper **inlay** with an inlay made from alkaline bristol.
- Mount the trimmed original spine onto the new spine; smooth frayed corners with glue.

Cost
- Batch production at approximately 15 minutes per item.
- Materials cost approximately 25 cents per item.

Equipment and Supplies
- Board shear
- Book press
- Metal-edged pressing boards
- Cork-backed metal ruler
- Embroidery or surgical scissors
- Scalpel
- Spatula
- Glue brush
- Bone folder
- Bookcloth and buckram (assorted colors, precut 30 cm by the width of the **bolt** or purchased precut in rolls)
- Super cloth (precut in various widths)
- Inlays (lightweight alkaline bristol, precut widths in 3-mm increments)
- Polyester grosgrain ribbon, 3 mm wide
- Polyvinyl acetate (PVA) adhesive (dilute 3:1, PVA:water)
- Pressure-sensitive tape, 2 cm wide
- Wastepaper

Operating Procedures—Typical Sequence
1. Select a book for repair when the cover's hinges are torn but the cover is in relatively good condition and the text block is still attached to its case with super and endsheets intact (photo 1).
2. Remove the original spine.
   a. Place a metal ruler just past the hinge on the cover board and slit through the cloth with a scalpel (photo 2).
   b. Open the cover and make slits 2.5 cm from the hinge where the turn-ins meet the endsheet (photo 3).
   c. Use embroidery scissors to snip cloth at the head and tail to release the spine completely.
   d. Repeat for the other cover board.
3. Use a spatula to help peel the bookcloth 2.5 cm off the cover boards (photo 4). To avoid creasing the lifted cloth, hold it back with a strip of tape.

4. Peel the original spine away from the inlay (photo 5) and **trim** it on the board shear so that all the frayed edges are removed and the original spine can be mounted evenly onto a new spine. Trim as little as possible to retain the original appearance of the spine.

5. Select the correct size inlay (photo 6) and trim it to the **height** of the cover boards. The width of the inlay must be *exactly* equal to the width of the spine of the text block. (For accuracy, measure the spine width with a flexible piece of paper rather than a rigid ruler).

6. Select bookcloth for the new spine from the precut pieces of bookcloth and cut to the width of the inlay plus 5 cm (photo 7).

7. From rolls of precut super, cut a piece of reinforcing cloth the height of the cover boards and tear it so its width is 1.5 cm wider than the inlay (photo 8).

8. Apply glue to the reinforcing cloth (photo 9), center it on the bookcloth (photo 10), and bone in place.

9. Apply glue to the inlay, center it on the bookcloth, and bone in place (photo 11). Trim the bookcloth hinges 2 cm on both sides of the inlay.

10. Cut a piece of 3-mm polyester ribbon the width of the inlay plus 1.5 cm.

11. Attach the polyester ribbon onto the inlay at the head of the cover (photo 12).

12. Using embroidery scissors, clip the bookcloth to the corners of the inlay to allow the cloth to be turned over the inlay 1.5 cm (photo 13). By clipping the bookcloth, the hinges that will be attached to the cover boards can be angled slightly, producing neater work (photo 14).

13. Shape the new spine piece by rubbing it lengthwise against a dowel rod or pole so that it will assume the curved shape of the spine (photo 15).

14. Lay strips of pressure-sensitive tape on the cover boards, score the edge slightly with a scalpel, and lift the tape to remove a layer of bookboard. Repeat two or three times. The layers that are removed will allow the new bookcloth to be *recessed* into the cover boards, avoiding a ridge when the original cloth is reattached.

15. Apply glue to one of the new bookcloth hinges (photo 16), place it on the cover board under the lifted original cloth, and bone in place (photo 17). Repeat for the other cover board.

16. Apply glue to the lifted original cloth (photo 18) and rub it down in place over the new cloth. Bone *over* a sheet of wastepaper to prevent "shining up" the cloth.

17. Apply glue to the original spine, position it carefully on the new spine (photo 20), and bone over a piece of paper.

18. Apply a little PVA where the cloth was slit at the head and tail of the cover boards, and smooth in place. Check the outside corners of the cover boards for frayed threads, glue sparingly, and smooth in place (photo 21). Bone in the hinges (photo 19).

19. Press the book between metal-edged boards in a book press for at least 15 minutes (photo 22).

Special Instructions

*   Bookcloth and buckram should be precut so that the **selvage** runs parallel with the spine of the book.
*   Use starch-filled or natural finish bookcloth or buckram. Pyroxylin coated cloths are harder to work with and do not accept a mounted spine. In general, the less textured side of the bookcloth is the *wrong* side, but there is a wide variety of finishes on bookcloth.
*   Super cloth is used to reinforce weak bookcloth in the vulnerable hinge area. When a heavier weight cloth is used, the reinforcing cloth is not necessary.
*   Inlays should be cut so that the grain direction of the bristol runs parallel with the length of the strip.
*   For speed and efficiency, work should be batched so that each step is performed for several books before moving to the next step.
*   If one or both endsheets are torn, but the super is intact, the damaged endsheets can be replaced. (See "Replacing a Torn Endsheet.")

- When the original spine is too deteriorated to be mounted, or is totally illegible, the new spine should be titled before attaching it to the book. (See "New Cover.")

NEW BOOKCLOTH SPINE WITH MOUNTED ORIGINAL SPINE

Illustrated

1 — Select for repair when a cover's hinges are torn or very weak.

2—Using a metal ruler and scalpel, slit through the cloth.

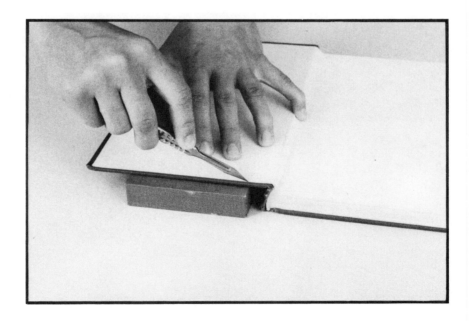

3—Open the cover and make slits, top and bottom.

4—Using a spatula, lift and peel the bookcloth back 2.5 cm.

5—Peel the original inlay away from the spine.

6 — Select a new inlay.

7 — Select bookcloth for a new spine and cut.

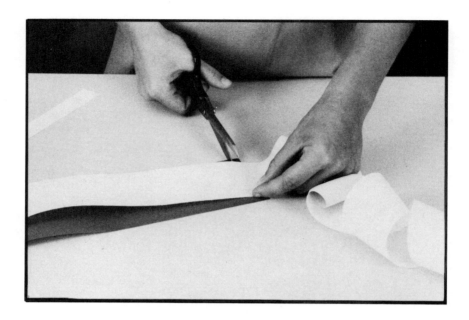

8 — Cut a piece of reinforcing cloth.

9 — Apply glue to the reinforcing cloth.

10—Center the reinforcing cloth on the new spine piece.

11—Attach the inlay to the new spine piece.

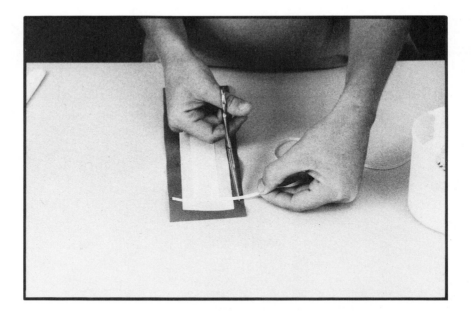

12—Attach the polyester ribbon at the top of the inlay.

13—Clip the bookcloth to the corners of the inlay.

14 — Turn over the cloth onto the inlay, angling the sides slightly.

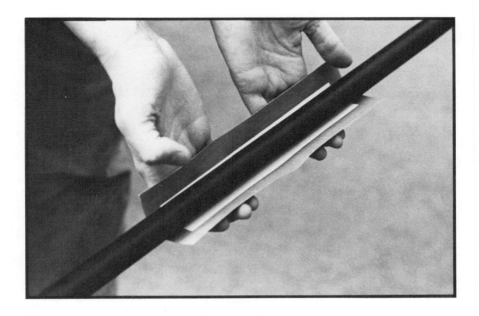

15 — Shape the new spine piece.

16 — Apply glue to one of the new bookcloth hinges.

17 — Bone the new spine piece in place under the lifted original cloth.

18—Apply glue to the lifted original cloth.

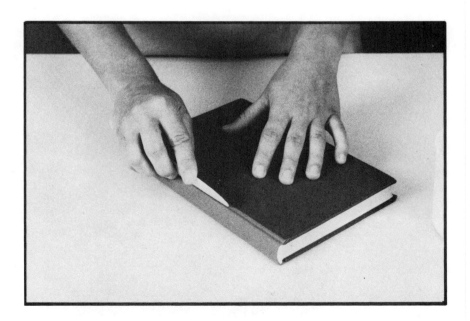

19—Reattach the original cloth to the cover boards.

20—Mount the original spine onto the new spine.

21—Apply a little PVA to frayed corners and smooth in place.

22 — Press the book between metal-edged boards in a book press.

RECASING USING THE ORIGINAL COVER

Problem
- Text block detached from its cover.
- Torn endsheets and torn super in the inside hinge area.

Causes
- Normal wear and tear from frequent use.
- Improper shelving practices, especially leaning books or fore-edge shelving.
- Careless or rough handling or dropping.
- Damaging book return systems.
- Inattention to loose hinges.
- Inadequate publisher's bindings, including weak cheesecloth-like super or no super.
- Inadequate binding for the weight of the book.
- Inadequate rounding and backing or a flat-back spine.

Treatment
- Recase the text block into its original cover after replacing deteriorated, damaged, or inadequate components.
  - Replace torn endsheets with alkaline endsheets.
  - Replace weak super with strong, tightly-woven super.
  - Reinforce the shape of the spine by applying a flexible adhesive and new spine linings.
  - Make minor repairs to the cloth case, including reinforcing weak cloth at the head and tail, replacing a worn inlay, and treating frayed edges with glue.

Cost
- Batch production at approximately 25 minutes per item.
- Materials cost approximately 20 cents per item.

Equipment and Supplies
- Board shear
- Book press
- Metal-edged pressing boards
- Scissors
- Scalpel
- Cork-backed metal ruler
- Kitchen knife
- Glue brush
- Bone folder
- Bookcloth (assorted colors)
- Endsheets (alkaline, single-fold in precut sizes)
- Goyu or Sekishu (Japanese paper) strips, 2 cm wide
- Super cloth (precut in various widths)
- Inlays (light-weight alkaline bristol, precut widths in 3-mm increments)
- **Blotting paper**, white
- Polyvinyl acetate (PVA) adhesive (dilute 3:1, PVA:water)
- Mixture of PVA and starch paste (3:1)
- Wastepaper
- Waxed paper
- Scrap piece of board

Operating Procedures—Typical Sequence
1. Select a book for repair when the book's endsheets and super are torn in the hinge.
2. Release the text block from its cover by easing the tipped-on fly leaf away from the text block and then slitting the super to release the text block completely (photo 1). If the book was sewn over tapes, the tapes should be freed from the cover, taking care not to disturb the sewing.

3. Strip the old super off the cover (photo 2) and sand lightly so that new endsheets will go on smoothly. If necessary, reattach or replace the inlay.

4. Clean the spine of the text block. Remove old cloth and kraft paper linings (photo 3). It is not necessary to clean the spine completely, but only to remove loose or deteriorated material.

5. Cut super for the spine 6 mm shorter than the text block and 5 cm wider than the spine (photo 4).

6. Select new endsheets slightly larger than the text block. Using mixture, attach a 2-cm strip of Goyu or Sekishu to the fold of each endsheet to act as a hinge. To attach the hinges:
   a. Lay the folds of the endsheets between strips of wastepaper leaving exposed a 1-cm width the entire length of the endsheet.
   b. Apply glue to the folds (photo 5).
   c. Place *half* of the width of the strip over each pasted area and pat in place (photo 6).
   d. Bend the other half of the strip around the fold and lay the folds of both endsheets between strips of blotting paper under a light, even weight until dry (photo 7).

7. Measure (photo 8) and trim the endsheets to the exact height of the text block.

8. Tip on the hinged endsheets.
   a. Place the hinges between strips of wastepaper and apply mixture (photo 9).
   b. Position the endsheet over the text block and carefully lower it so that the hinge fits into the shoulder and the folded edge lines up exactly with the first (or last) section of the book (photo 10).
   c. Bone the endsheet against the shoulder (photo 11). The hinge should be attached to the text block and the endsheet should swing freely at the fold.
   d. *Immediately* place waxed paper between the hinge and the endsheet to prevent sticking (photo 12).

9. Trim the endsheet to the exact width of the text block using a ruler and scalpel, and cutting on a scrap piece of board.

10. Apply PVA generously to the spine of the text block (photo 13), position the super with approximately 2.5 cm on either side, and **rub** and bone securely down (photo 14).

11. Measure (photo 15) and cut a spine strip from scrap endsheet paper the width of the spine and 3 mm shorter than book height. The grain direction of the paper should run parallel with the spine. Apply mixture to the strip, position it carefully, and rub and bone securely down (photo 16).

12. Case in the text block.
    a. Position the text block on the open cover. Check again, it is easy to case the book in upside down!
    b. Brushing vertically from the center out, glue the hinge of the super to the endsheet with mixture (photo 17). Continue brushing until the entire front endsheet is evenly covered.
    c. Carefully close the cover and bone in the hinge (photo 18). Be sure the spine of the text block is pushed back all the way against the spine of the cover.
    d. While supporting the text block, open the front cover so that the spine lies over the edge of the table and the hinge meets the rim. Smooth the endsheet by rubbing with a soft cloth or boning *over* a piece of wastepaper (photo 19). Do not open the cover more than 140 degrees or the endsheet will stretch, causing a crease in the joint.
    e. Repeat step 12 for the back of the book.

13. Place waxed paper between the folds of the endsheets and press the book between metal-edged pressing boards in a book press (photo 20).

Special Instructions
- There are many different styles of endsheets and methods for attaching them, including simple tipping on, sewing on through the fold, and hinging on (illustrated in this manual).

For more information see item 34 of the Bibliography. In addition, it is often desirable to save the original endsheets, especially when they contain illustrative materials.

- If the cloth in the hinge area of the cover is seriously weakened, a reinforcing strip of new bookcloth should be attached to the inside of the spine. The bookcloth should extend approximately 1.5 cm onto the cover boards and also reinforce the turn-ins at the head and tail. See "Lining the Spine of an Original Cover" for details.
- If the cloth at the head and tail is weak or torn but the bookcloth in the hinge area is strong, small slips of matching bookcloth can be inserted on the *inside* of the cover at the head and tail, and the inlay replaced.
- After recasing, the book should open with very little or no drag on the first few pages. This requires *exact* placement of the endsheets when they are tipped on.

RECASING USING THE ORIGINAL COVER

Illustrated

1—Release the text block from its cover.

2—Strip the old super off the cover.

3—Clean the spine of the text block.

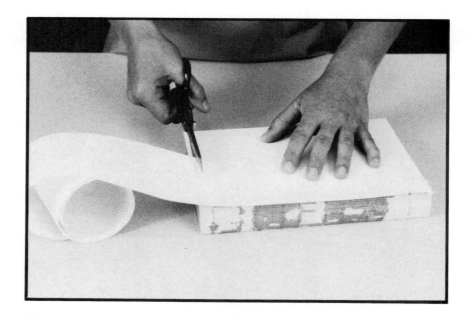

4—Cut new super.

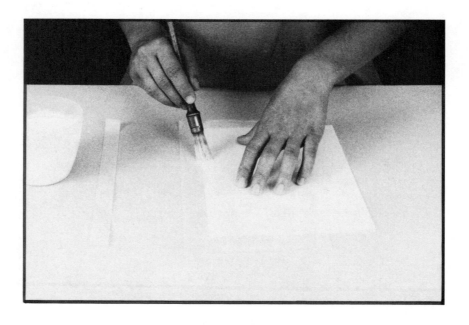

5—Apply mixture to the folds of the endsheets.

6 — Position the strip so that its center is over the fold.

7 — Weight the folds between blotters until dry.

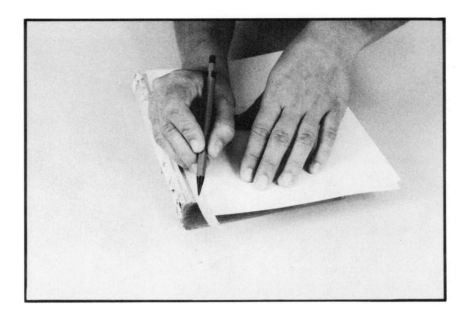

8 — Measure the endsheets to the exact height of the text block.

9 — Apply mixture to the hinge.

10—Position the endsheet over the text block.

11—Bone the endsheet against the shoulder of the text block.

12—Place waxed paper between the hinge and the endsheet.

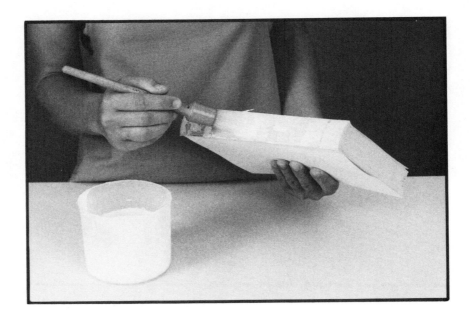

13—Apply glue to the spine.

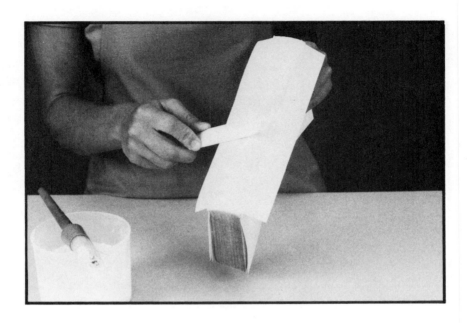

14 — Attach the super to the spine.

15 — Measure a spine strip.

16 — Attach the spine strip.

17 — Attach the hinge of the super to the endsheet.

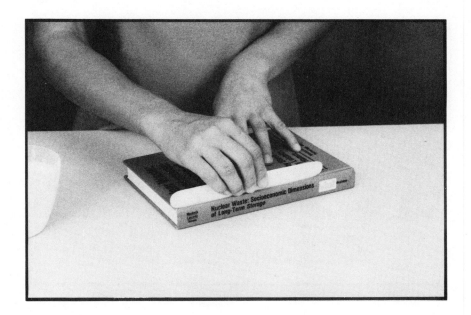

18—Bone in the hinge.

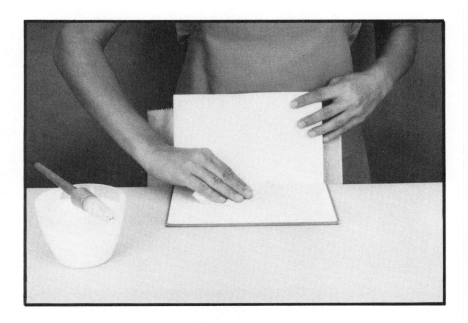

19—Smooth the endsheet.

20 — Press the book between metal-edged pressing boards in a book press.

LINING THE SPINE OF AN ORIGINAL COVER

Problem
- Torn or seriously weakened cloth in the hinge area of a cover *combined with* torn super in the inside hinge area or a detached text block.

Causes
- Normal wear and tear from frequent use.
- Improper shelving practices.
- Damage to the spine from exposure to ultraviolet light in sunlight or fluorescent light.

Treatment
- Line the *inside* of the spine of the original cover with a matching piece of new bookcloth and replace the inlay. This repair is *preceded* by releasing the cover from its text block and *followed* by recasing the text block into the original cover after adding new endsheets and spine linings. (See "Recasing Using the Original Cover.")

Cost
- Batch production at approximately 35 minutes per item.
- Materials cost approximately 35 cents per item.

Equipment and Supplies
- Board shear
- Book press
- Metal-edged boards
- Cork-backed metal ruler
- Scissors
- Scalpel
- Glue brush
- Kitchen knife
- Bone folder
- Bookcloth (assorted colors)
- Endsheets (alkaline, single-fold in precut sizes)
- Goyu or Sekishu (Japanese paper) strips, 2 cm wide
- Super cloth (precut in various widths)
- Inlays (light-weight alkaline bristol, precut widths in 3-mm increments)
- Polyester grosgrain ribbon, 3 mm wide
- Blotting paper, white
- Polyvinyl acetate (PVA) adhesive (dilute 3:1, PVA:water)
- Mixture of PVA and starch paste (3:1)
- Wastepaper
- Waxed paper
- Scrap piece of pressboard

Operating Procedures — Typical Sequence
1. Select a book for repair when the spine of the cover is torn or deteriorated, and endsheets and super in the inside hinge area are torn.
2. Release the text block from its cover, remove old endsheets and spine linings, and replace with new materials following steps 2 through 11 of "Recasing Using the Original Cover."
3. Strip the old super off the cover and sand lightly so that the new endsheets will go on smoothly.
4. With the inside of the cover facing up, use a scalpel to slit through the turn-ins 2.5 cm onto the cover boards on either side of the spine (photo 1). The slits will allow the turn-ins to be peeled back.
5. Peel the old inlay away from the spine (photo 2).
6. Slowly peel the covering material away from the cover boards until it is even with the slits in the turn-ins (photo 3). Take care not to rip weakened cloth in the hinge area.

7. Select the correct size inlay and trim it to the height of the cover boards. The width of the inlay must be *exactly* equal to the width of the spine of the text block with its *new* spine linings attached (photo 4).

8. Select matching bookcloth to line the spine and cut to the width of the inlay plus 5 cm (photo 5). The length of the cloth lining should be equal to the height of the cover boards plus 5 cm.

9. Hold the cover so that the spine and the peeled back covering material are exposed and apply glue (photo 6). Work quickly and use glue *sparingly*.

10. Position the new cloth spine lining over the glued area and pat gently in place (photo 7). Lower the cover and bone the lining gently against the original spine (photo 8).

11. Flip the cover right side up and smooth frayed threads in place with the fingers. Wipe away any excess glue.

12. Apply glue to the cover boards where they were peeled back from the covering material (photo 9). Flip the cover right side up, and bone the original cloth down over a protective piece of scrap paper.

13. Apply glue to the inlay, center on the inside of the spine (photo 10), and bone in place.

14. Cut a piece of 3-mm polyester ribbon the width of the inlay plus 1.5 cm (photo 11). Attach the polyester ribbon to the inlay at the head of the cover.

15. Trim the new cloth spine lining even with the original turn-ins at the head and tail.

16. Apply glue to the turn-ins and reattach onto the inlay (photo 12).

17. Shape the spine by rubbing it lengthwise against a dowel rod or pole until it assumes the proper curved shape.

18. Case in the text block and press the book following steps 12 and 13 of "Recasing Using the Original Cover."

Special Instructions

- If a substantial amount of the cloth in the hinge area is worn away or missing, a new spine should be constructed and the original spine trimmed and mounted onto the new spine.

LINING THE SPINE OF AN ORIGINAL COVER

Illustrated

1 — Slit through the turn-ins on either side of the spine.

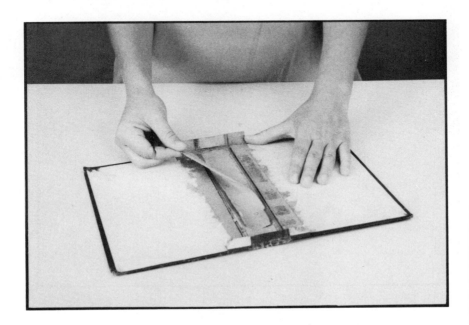

2 — Peel the old inlay away from the spine.

3—Peel the covering material away from the cover boards.

4—Select the correct size inlay.

5 — Cut matching bookcloth to line the spine.

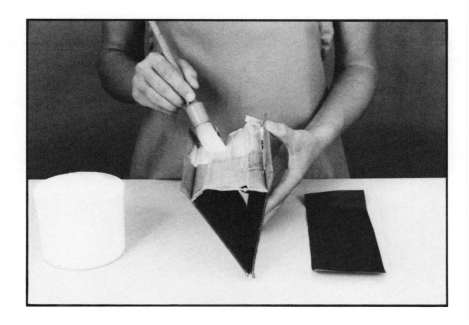

6 — Apply glue to the exposed original spine.

7— Position the new cloth spine lining over the glued area and pat in place.

8— Bone the lining gently against the original spine.

9—Apply glue to the cover boards where they were peeled back from the covering material.

10—Center the inlay on the spine and bone in place.

11—Cut a piece of polyester ribbon to reinforce the head.

12—Reattach the turn-ins to the inlay.

REATTACHING LOOSE SECTIONS

Problem
- A section(s) has loosened or detached from a Smyth-sewn text block, especially at the front or back of the book.

Causes
- Original sewing thread was too thin for the weight of the text block.
- Stress to the text block due to improper shelving, especially shelving on the fore-edge.
- Damage to sewing threads when spine is exposed and in need of repair.
- Uneven tension or missed links in the original sewing structure.

Treatment
- Attach loose or detached sections to secure sections by sewing with linen thread.

Cost
- Approximately 1 minute per loose section.
- Materials cost negligible per section.

Equipment and Supplies
- Sewing needle with large eye
- Unbleached linen thread
- Scissors, embroidery or surgical

Operating Procedures—Typical Sequence
1. Select a book for repair when a section(s) has pulled away from the text block or when the original sewing structure is loose or damaged (photo 1).
2. Thread a needle with linen thread cut the height of the text block multiplied by the number of sections to be sewn *plus* one.
3. Prepare a secure section for linking to the first loose or detached section. Sewing should begin with the outermost section that is still firmly attached to the text block.
   a. Bring the threaded needle through the first original sewing hole at the top of the text block, and back out of the section at the second hole. Leave a 4-cm tail at the beginning.
   b. Form a loop at each hole by exiting and entering the same hole along the length of the spine. It is not necessary to use all of the original sewing holes; select holes for sewing "stations" spaced approximately 3 cm apart, depending on the size and weight of the text block (photo 2).
   c. At the end of the section, exit the last sewing hole to the outside.
4. Link the loose section to the first secure section.
   a. Position the sections with the sewing holes lined up.
   b. Enter the loose section at the first original sewing hole at the *bottom* of the text block.
   c. Exit at the sewing hole that corresponds to the first loop and bring the thread up through the loop and back into the section through the same sewing hole so the loops are interlocked (photo 3). Pull the thread *in the direction of the sewing*; thread pulled opposite the sewing direction will tear the fold of the section.
   d. Repeat previous step for each loop.
   e. Exit the first sewing hole at the top of the text block and tie the thread in a square knot with the tail from the beginning of the sewing. If only one section needs to be secured, this is the final step. If there is another loose section, continue sewing without cutting the thread (fig. 2.1).
5. Position the second loose section on the text block with the sewing holes lined up. Enter the section at the first sewing hole at the top of the section, exit at the second sewing hole, and bring the thread *behind* the new stitching and back into the section. Continue linking the stitches at each sewing section.
6. At the end of the section, loop the thread behind the stitch below it. If sewing is to continue, enter the next section.

7. At the end of the final section, secure the sewing by making a loop around the last chain stitch and coming up through the loop to make a knot. Repeat (photo 4).

Special Instructions

*   In general, this procedure will not give the strength and support necessary for a large text block and should only be used for one or two sections.
*   Chain stitching may be used to secure an entire text block of it has only a few sections.
*   Endsheets can be chain stitched onto a text block using this method.
*   Weak folds of loose sections should be mended before sewing. See "Mending with Japanese Paper and Starch Paste."

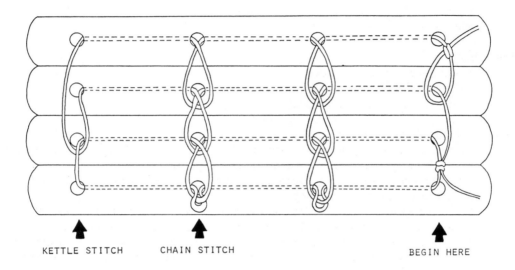

KETTLE STITCH   CHAIN STITCH   BEGIN HERE

Fig. 2.1. Sections chain-stitched together.

REATTACHING LOOSE SECTIONS

Illustrated

1 — Select a book for repair when the sections have loosened or detached.

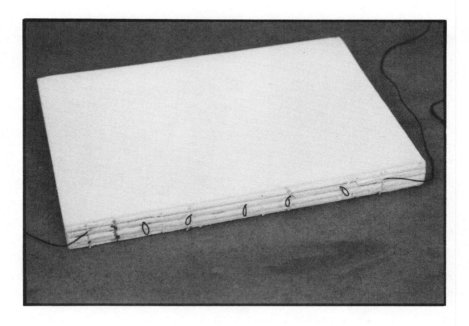

2 — Form loops at the sewing stations. [Ed. note: black thread was used to highlight the sewing structure; linen thread is tan.]

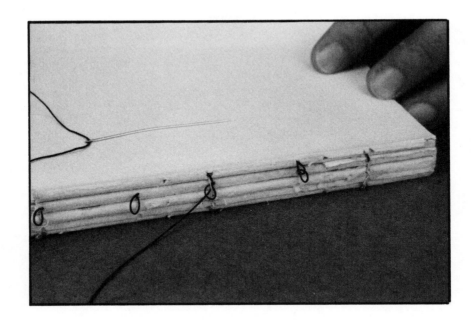

3—Connect sections with interlocking stitches.

4—The sewing must be secure before repairs to the book can resume.

NEW COVER

Problem
- Seriously deteriorated cover; text block and sewing still intact.
  - Hinges torn or weakened.
  - Corners bent, exposed, and frayed.
  - Headcap or tail torn or missing.
  - Lettering illegible or spine missing altogether.
- Cover detached from the text block and endsheets torn.
- Paper too fragile to withstand machine casing in methods used by commercial library binders; or the content, age, or format of the item makes it unsuitable for ordinary commercial library binding.
- Book has deteriorated components:
  - Acidic endsheets have embrittled the title page.
  - Spine linings have deteriorated, glue has dried out, and super is detached.

Causes
- Deterioration from exposure to excessive heat and humidity, atmospheric pollutants, and ultraviolet light rays.
- Improper storage or abuse over many years.
- Aging of component materials such as cloth, glue, leather, paper, endsheets, etc.
- Normal wear and tear from frequent use.

Treatment
- Recase the text block into a new cover:
  - Replace deteriorated endsheets, super and spine linings with new, strong materials.
  - Construct a compatible new cover using starch-filled bookcloth or buckram, and an alkaline inlay and cover boards.
  - Stamp the new cover with author and title information.

Cost
- Batch production at approximately 50 minutes per item.
- Materials cost approximately $1.00 per item.

Equipment and Supplies
- Board shear
- Book press
- Metal-edged pressing boards
- Stamping press with typeholder, or with chase, pallets, and furniture; type cabinet; type
- Electrician's clamps, rubber-tipped
- Tweezers
- **Stamping foil** (various colors)
- Oven mitt
- Pressure-sensitive tape
- Cork-backed metal ruler
- Scissors
- Scalpel
- Kitchen knife
- Glue brush
- Bone folder
- Polyvinyl acetate (PVA) adhesive (dilute 3:1, PVA:water)
- Mixture of PVA and starch paste, 1:3
- Inlays (lightweight, alkaline bristol, precut widths in 3-mm increments)
- Bookboard ("Acid-pHree" Davey Red Label, caliper .060, .082, .098)
- Bookcloth and buckram (starch-filled in assorted colors)
- Goyu or Sekishu (Japanese paper) strips, 2 cm wide
- Endsheets (alkaline, single-fold in precut sizes)
- Blotting paper, white

- Super cloth (precut in various widths)
- Wastepaper
- Waxed paper
- Scrap piece of board

Operating Procedures — Typical Sequence

1. Select a book for a new cover when the original cover is beyond simple repair and the item is not suitable for restoration or commercial library binding (photo 1).
2. Release the text block from its cover by easing the tipped-on fly leaf away from the text block and then slitting the super to release the text block completely. If the book was sewn over tapes, the tapes should be freed from the cover, taking care not to disturb the sewing.
3. Clean the spine of the text block. Remove the old cloth and Kraft paper linings. Deteriorated **animal glue** on the spine should be removed.
    a. Prepare a thick starch paste or methyl cellulose paste.
    b. Brush the paste on the partially cleaned spine (photo 2) and allow the paste to soften the cloth and adhesive residue. Check to make sure the paste does not stand too long or the backs of the sections will soak up too much water.
    c. Using the blunt side of a kitchen knife, *gently* scrape off the softened glue and cloth (photo 3). Scrape *very* gently to avoid damaging the backs of the sections.
    d. This method of cleaning the spine does *not* work if synthetic adhesives such as PVA were used originally.
4. Replace endsheets and spine linings following steps 5 through 11 of "Recasing Using the Original Cover."
5. Measure and cut cover boards. The boards should fit against the shoulder made by the convex shape of the spine (the shape formed when the text block is rounded and backed) (photo 4). The **square** of the book (the part of the cover that extends beyond the text block to protect the edges of the paper) should be 3 mm wide at the head, tail, and fore-edge. The grain direction of the book board should run parallel with the spine of the book.
6. Select the correct size inlay and trim it to the height of the cover boards. The width of the inlay must be *exactly* equal to the width of the spine of the text block with its *new* spine linings attached. (For accuracy, measure the width with a flexible piece of paper rather than a rigid ruler.)
7. Cut a rectangle of cloth for the cover, allowing 2 cm turn-ins and hinges of 6 mm (fig. 2.2). The selvage should run parallel with the spine of the book.

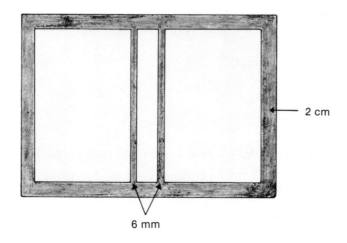

2 cm

6 mm

Fig. 2.2. Cut a rectangle of bookcloth for the cover.

8. Attach the inlay to the covering material (photo 5).
9. Set **type** for stamping the spine of the cover.
   a. Plan the author and title layout (fig. 2.3).
   b. Based on the longest line to be stamped and the spine width, choose a type size.
   c. Set each line into a pallet with the grooves on the type facing up, and spelling from right to left, assuming that the pallet is held as shown (photo 6). Even out the spacing between the letters (ens, ems). Fill out the pallet on either side of the type with *equal* spacing (quads) (photo 7).
   d. Place the pallets into the chase and arrange the furniture for line spacing to correspond with the stamping layout (photo 8).
   e. Lock the pallet and furniture into the chase, flip, and insert the chase into the head of the press (photo 9). Lock in place.
   f. Make a **blind stamp** (without foil) on a scrap piece of bookboard to check spelling, word spacing, letter spacing, and line spacing.
10. Stamp the spine.
    a. Preheat the press, chase, and type to 250-300 degrees Fahrenheit.
    b. Tape the covering material to a scrap piece of bookboard.
    c. Clamp the scrap piece of bookboard with the attached covering material to the bed of the press so that the material will not move as it is stamped. (The center of the spine should line up exactly with the center of the bed.)
    d. Determine the vertical position of the stamping on the spine, position the bed, and lock in place.
    e. Blind stamp the spine.
    f. Stamp with **foil** (shiny side up) two to five times. The letters should be evenly filled in (photo 10).
    g. Repeat the blind stamp
11. Clean up the stamped area with a soft cloth and Magic Rub® pencil eraser so that the stamped letters are distinct (photo 11).
12. Remove the chase from the press, allow it to cool, and **distribute the type**.
13. Attach the cover boards to the covering material (photo 12), trim the corners (fig. 2.4), and turn in the excess material onto the cover boards (photo 13).

Ingersoll's Famous Speeches

Fig. 2.3. Plan the author and title layout for the spine.

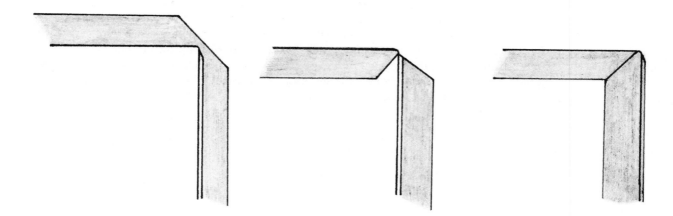

Fig. 2.4. Form the corners of the new cover.

14. Case in the text block and press the book following steps 11 through 13 of "Recasing Using the Original Cover."

Special Instructions

- The explanation of stamping in this procedure is *grossly oversimplified* and includes only information necessary to stamp for routine book repair or protective enclosure. A serious student of bookbinding or conservation will require an *in-depth* exposure to typography, printing, composition, and stamping techniques.

- A stamping press, type, type cabinet, and accouterments represent a substantial investment for a library. Once assembled, however, ongoing costs are negligible and the variety and quality of conservation work that can be performed is greatly enhanced.

- Stamping occurs when heated type is pressed against stamping foil and *impressed* into the material to be stamped. The stamping technique combines heat, pressure, and dwell (the length of time that type and foil remain in contact with the material being stamped). These three elements are manipulated by the operator depending on the type of material being stamped, the stamping foil, the length of a line or the total number of lines, the size of the type, and the operator's technique or "touch." Some individuals prefer higher temperatures and light, and quick pressure, while others get better results with lower temperatures and harder pressure applied for longer periods of time. Like any manual procedure, craftsmanlike stamping comes with experience. For a discussion of stamping foils see item 35 of the Bibliography.

- There are many manufacturers of stamping machines, but hand-operated machines are only a fraction of the stamping industry. Some stamping machines feature a self-centering typeholder attached to the head of the press. The typeholder tilts up to allow the type to be set. Generally, one line is stamped at a time, and the bed of the press is moved to position each new line. More expensive stamping machines allow several lines to be stamped at the same time. Each line is set into individual self-centering pallets that are placed into a chase. The spacing between the lines is determined by the placement of aluminum "furniture" between the lines. Pallets and furniture are secured into the chase, and the chase is flipped and locked into the head of the press. Used machines are often available because commercial binderies have largely switched to computer-driven stamping equipment.

- Type for hand book work can be made from brass, steel, or a metal alloy. Service Type®, an alloy, is often used because it is less expensive than either brass or steel and works well for most stamping operations. Libraries adding stamping capabilities to their repertoire may want to invest in one or two standard type faces in several sizes. The size of type is expressed in points. A point is approximately 1/72 of an inch. A common point size is 12 point or a pica. Typical type sizes for book work are 10 point, 12 point, 14 point, and 18 point. Type is sold in fonts. A **font** contains an assortment of letters in one size and style. The quantity of each letter depends on the frequency of its use.

- For speed in stamping several books with different titles, the chase can be preheated while the type is being set. An oven mitt is then used to hold and flip the chase.

- Starch-filled bookcloth and buckram are preferred over pyroxylin or acrylic-coated cloths because they are easier to work with and more attractive, although not more durable.

- There is a great deal of variation in book structure, thus a hinge 6 mm will not be correct for *every* book.

NEW COVER

Illustrated

1 — Select for a new cover when the original cover is beyond simple repair and the item is not suitable for commercial library binding or restoration.

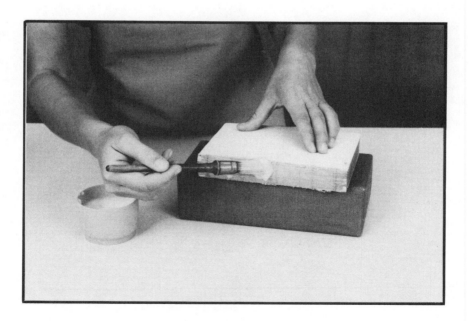

2 — Brush thick paste on the partially cleaned spine.

3 — Gently scrape off the softened adhesive and cloth residue.

4 — New cover boards should fit against the shoulder made by the convex shape of the spine.

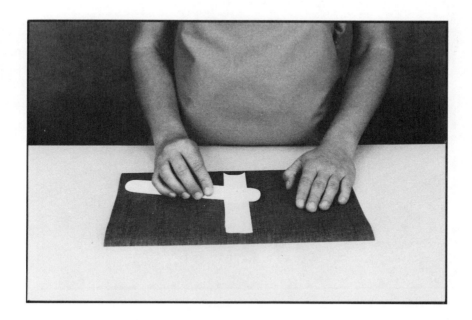

5—Attach the inlay to the covering material.

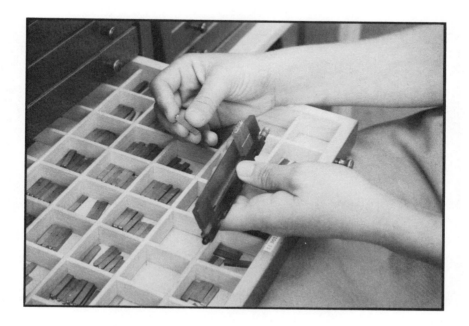

6—Set the type into the pallet.

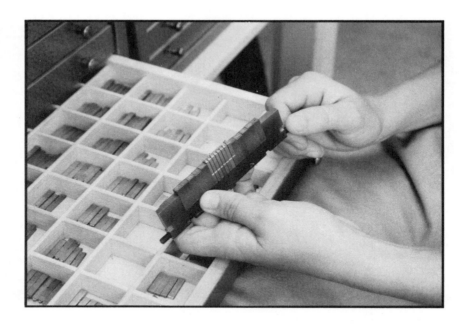

7 — Fill out the pallet on either side of the type with equal spacing.

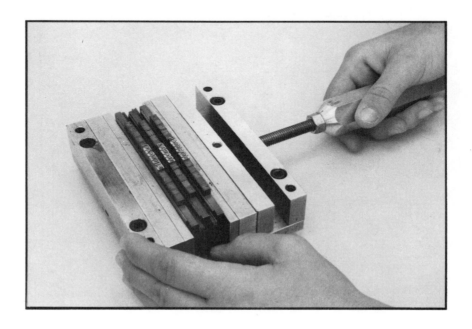

8 — Arrange the pallets and furniture in the chase.

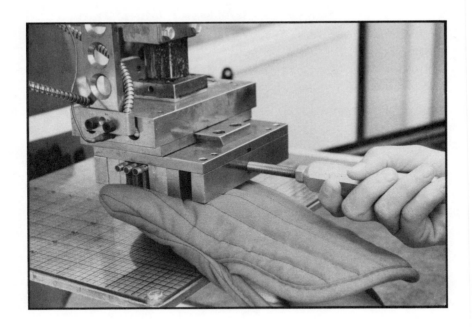

9—Insert the chase into the head of the press.

10—Stamp the spine.

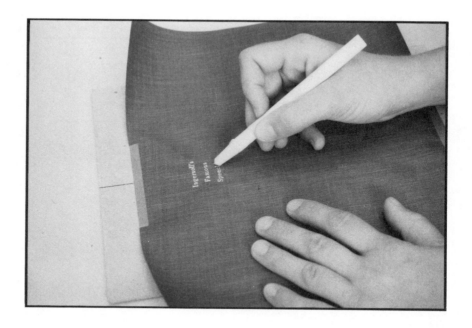

11—Clean up the stamped area.

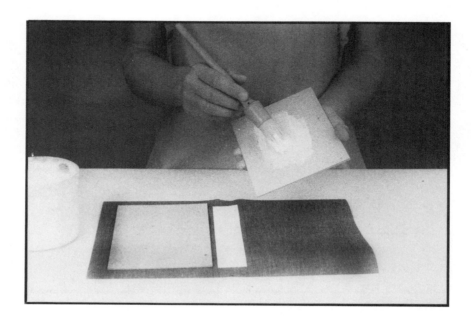

12—Attach the cover boards to the covering material.

13—Turn the excess covering material onto the boards.

14—Be sure the spine of the text block is pushed all the way back against the spine of the cover.

15 — Bone in the hinge.

16 — Press the book until dry.

3
Maintenance Procedures

PAMPHLET BINDING

Problem
- Unbound single-section pamphlet needing protection prior to circulation or use.

Causes
- Flexible paper cover becomes soiled and worn if the item does not have a protective cover.
- Title page can be damaged if the paper cover is detached and lost.

Treatment
- Provide a simple in-house binding to protect the pamphlet from unnecessary wear and tear:
  - Construct a simple binder with boxboard covers and a buckram spine.
  - Use an alkaline endsheet for further protection.
  - Sew the pamphlet into the binder with linen thread.

Cost
- Batch production at approximately 15 minutes per item.
- Materials cost approximately 75 cents per item.

Equipment and Supplies
- Board shear
- Awls (thin, needle size)
- Scissors
- Ruler
- Staple remover
- Oyster knife
- Sewing needle with large eye
- Corner rounder (1/8-inch diameter cutting blade)
- Glue brush
- Bone folder
- Endsheets (alkaline, single-fold in precut sizes)
- Unbleached linen thread
- Polyvinyl acetate (PVA) adhesive (dilute 2:1, PVA:water)
- Buckram strips (precut 7 cm wide or purchased in precut rolls)
- Boxboard (alkaline, caliper .040, .052, .060)
- Wrapped fire brick
- Envelopes (alkaline)
- Empty one-pound coffee can to hold sewing thread (bring the thread up through a hole in the center of the lid)
- Waxed paper
- Wastepaper

Operating Procedures—Typical Sequence
1. Select a single-section item for pamphlet binding (photo 1) and remove the staples. Use a staple remover, or for difficult cases pry the staples open with an oyster knife.

2. Select a folded endsheet slightly larger than the pamphlet (photo 2) and trim it to the same size as the pamphlet.
3. Cut two cover boards from alkaline boxboard 3 mm narrower and 6 mm longer than the pamphlet (photo 3). The grain of the board should run parallel with the spine of pamphlet.
4. Using a corner rounder, round the fore-edge corners of the cover boards to prevent "dog ears" (photo 4).
5. Cut two buckram strips for the spine from precut rolls of buckram. The length of the inner strip should be equal to the height of the pamphlet. The outer strip should be 4 cm longer than the pamphlet (photo 5).
6. Fold the inner strip in half lengthwise with right sides together (photo 6).
7. Holding the pamphlet open to the center and using three awls, pierce evenly spaced holes through the pamphlet, endsheet, and buckram strip (photo 7). The holes should be 3 or 4 cm apart, depending on the height of the pamphlet (usually three, five, or seven holes).
8. Thread a needle with a length of linen thread twice the height of the pamphlet.
9. Remove the center awl. Begin sewing from the outside (photo 8), and sew the pamphlet to the buckram strip in a figure-eight pattern (fig. 3.1), removing awls as necessary and pulling the thread taut *in the direction of the sewing* to prevent tearing the paper (photo 9).

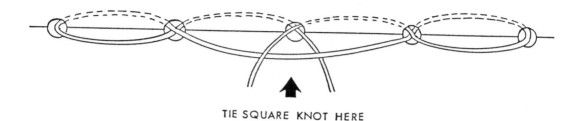

TIE SQUARE KNOT HERE

Fig. 3.1. Sew the pamphlet to the buckram strip in a figure-eight pattern.

10. Tie a square knot on the outside of the buckram strip (photo 10) and secure with a dab of glue.
11. Sandwich the pamphlet between the cover boards leaving a 6-mm inner hinge at the sewn edge. The square of the boards should equal 3 mm at the head, tail, and fore-edge. Fold the outer buckram strip around the spine of the pamphlet and mark the front cover board at the edge of the buckram strip (photo 11). Remove the pamphlet and set it aside.
12. Construct the pamphlet binder.
    a. Place the marked cover board between two sheets of wastepaper and apply glue to the area that will be covered by the buckram strip.
    b. Position the buckram strip over the glued area (photo 12) and bone in place.
    c. Flip the cover board wrong side up and measure a gap for the spine equal to the thickness of the pamphlet plus 12 mm.
    d. Apply glue to the rest of the buckram strip and position the second cover board up to the marks (photo 13). Be sure to line up the bottom edges of the cover boards.
    e. Flip the pamphlet binder right side up and bone the buckram strip in place.
    f. Flip the binder wrong side up, apply glue to the excess cloth at the head and tail, and turn it over onto the cover boards (photo 14). Use a bone folder to crease the cloth.
13. Center the pamphlet in the cover and apply glue to the outside of one side of the inner buckram strip (photo 15). Carefully bone the strip against the cover, especially in the hinge area. Repeat for the other side (photo 16).
14. Close the cover and bone in the hinge (photo 17). Place waxed paper between the cover and the endsheets and weight the binding until dry (photo 18).

Special Instructions

- Ready-made pamphlet binders can be purchased from commercial vendors, although the quality of materials and construction should be carefully considered. See *Equipment and Supplies* for sources. Pamphlet binding is also available as a service from commercial library binderies. A comparison of the cost of commercial binders and binding services with the cost of in-house pamphlet binding should be made. However, because some items will be needed immediately, some in-house binding will always be necessary.
- To save time, batch pamphlets and do at least five at a time.
- A typed label may be attached to the front of the binder. Spray the label with Krylon®, a plastic fixative, before attaching it to help keep the label clean.
- If necessary, damaged folds can be mended before binding the pamphlet. See "Mending with Japanese Paper and Starch Paste."
- When parts accompany musical scores, an endsheet should be sewn around each part, and the parts placed in a pocket at the back of the binder. The pocket can be constructed from alkaline folder stock or a commercially available alkaline envelope.
- Thin multiple-section pamphlets already sewn together through the folds can be bound by sewing the first and last sections to the inner buckram strip.

PAMPHLET BINDING

Illustrated

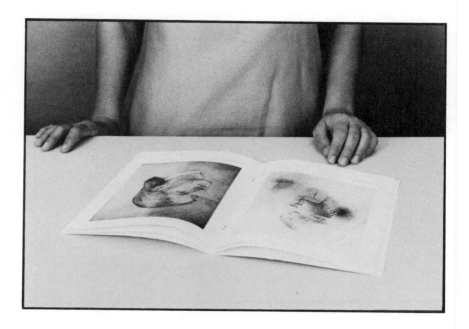

1 — Select a single-section item for pamphlet binding.

2—Select an endsheet slightly larger than the pamphlet.

3—Cut two cover boards from alkaline boxboard.

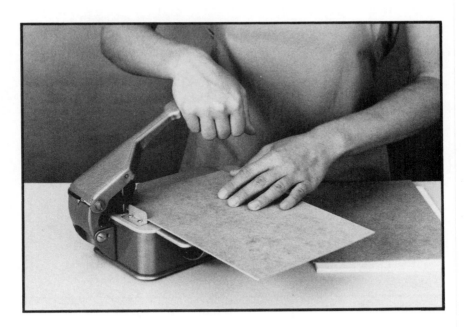

4—Round the fore-edge corners of the cover boards.

5—Cut two buckram strips for the spine.

6 — Fold the inner strip in half lengthwise.

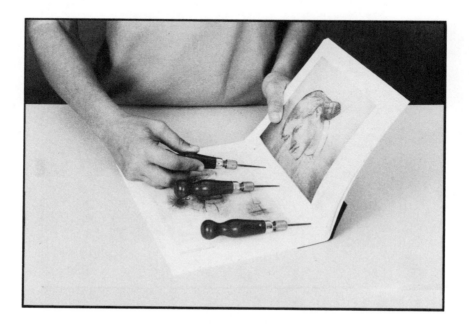

7 — Using three awls, pierce evenly spaced sewing holes.

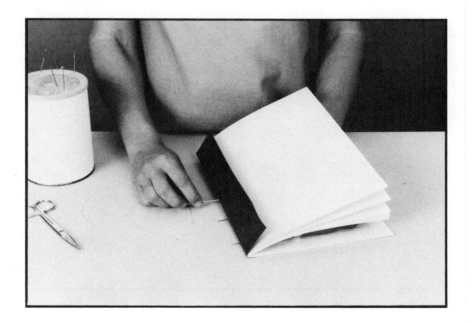

8 — Begin sewing from the outside, removing awls as necessary.

9 — Sew the pamphlet to the buckram strip in a figure-eight pattern.

10 — Tie a square knot on the outside.

11 — Fold the buckram strip around the spine of the pamphlet and mark the cover board.

12—Place the buckram strip over the glued area.

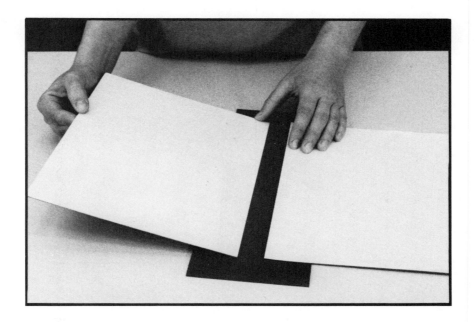

13—Position the second cover board on the buckram strip.

14—Turn over the excess cloth at the head and tail.

15—Apply glue to the inner buckram strip.

16—Bone the strip against the cover.

17—Close the cover and bone in the hinge.

18—Weight the pamphlet binding until dry.

PAPERBACK REINFORCEMENT

Problem
- A paperback book in need of protection prior to circulation or use:
  - A paperback book with coated paper that cannot be successfully adhesive-bound and is unsuitable for oversewing.
  - Viewing cover information is desirable.
  - A paperback with fold-out pages.
  - A paperback that is too thin for the paperback production line in a commercial library bindery.
  - A paperback with very narrow inner margins.

Causes
- Paper cover becomes worn and text block damaged if cover is not reinforced.

Treatment
- Reinforce the cover by adding cloth hinges to the inside joints and thin bristol boards to the inside of the paper covers.

Cost
- Batch production at approximately 5 minutes per item.
- Materials cost approximately 15 cents per item.

Equipment and Supplies
- Board shear
- Wrapped fire brick
- Scissors
- Ruler
- Glue brush
- Bone folder
- Bristol board (alkaline or pH neutral, caliper .020 or .030, precut into standard paperback sizes)
- **Cambric** hinge cloth, precut 2.5 cm wide
- Polyvinyl acetate (PVA) adhesive (dilute 2:1, PVA:water)
- Wastepaper
- Waxed paper

Operating Procedures—Typical Sequence
1. Select a paperback for reinforcement (photo 1).
2. Cut two pieces of reinforcing board and two cambric strips the exact height of the paperback. The grain of the board must run parallel with the spine of the paperback.
3. Gently pull the cover away from the first and last pages of the text block up to the edge of the spine (photo 2). Be careful not to detach the cover from the spine itself.
4. Apply glue to a cambric strip and place the strip on the inner hinge, half on the text block and half on the cover (photo 3).
5. Bone the cambric to ensure adhesion in the joint (photo 4).
6. Apply glue to one side of a piece of reinforcing board (photo 5).
7. On the inside of the cover, position the reinforcing board on top of the cambric strip, at the same time leaving a 6-mm inner hinge. Make sure the board is lined up with the top and bottom of the cover (photo 6).
8. Bone the cover to assure even adhesion between the cover and the reinforcing board (photo 7). Repeat steps 4 through 8 for the back cover.
9. Place waxed paper inside the cover and bone the outside hinge. Weight until dry (photo 8).
10. Trim excess reinforcing board even with the fore-edge of the book (photo 9).

Special Instructions
- This procedure is particularly useful when an item will be used infrequently, or when it is desirable to display the information printed on the cover. However, the result is only as

durable as the method of page attachment used by the publisher. A reinforced paperback cover will not prevent pages falling out due to deterioration of impermanent adhesives.

- To save time, batch paperbacks in groups of five.

PAPERBACK REINFORCEMENT

Illustrated

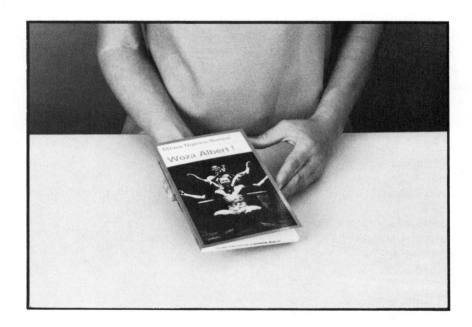

1—Select a paperback for reinforcement.

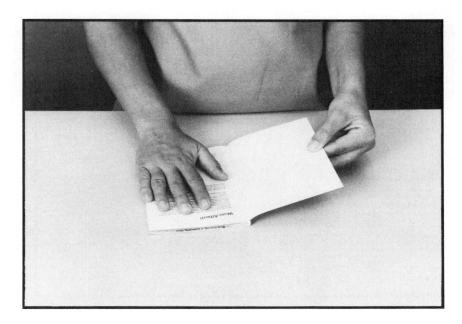

2 — Release the cover from the first and last page of the text block.

3 — Position the glue cambric strip on the hinge of the cover.

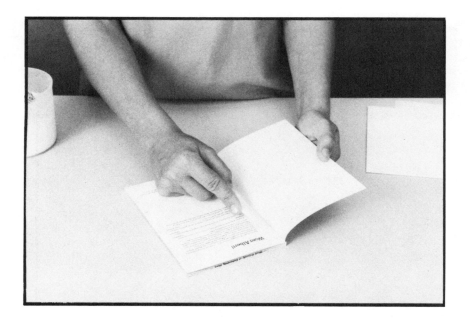

4 — Bone the cambric to ensure adhesion.

5 — Apply glue to the reinforcing board.

6 — Position the reinforcing board on the inside of the cover.

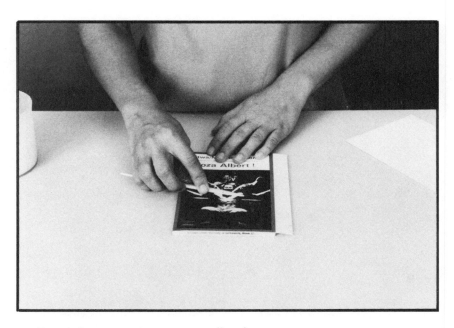

7 — Bone the cover to ensure adhesion.

8—Weight the book until dry.

9—Trim excess reinforcing board even with the fore-edge of the book.

PRESSBOARD REINFORCEMENT OF PAPERBACKS

Problem
- A paperback book in need of protection prior to circulation or use:
  - A paperback book that needs protection but cannot be sent to a commercial library bindery because it is needed immediately.
  - A paperback book with **coated paper** that cannot be successfully adhesive-bound and is unsuitable for oversewing.
  - A paperback with fold-out pages.
  - A paperback that is too thin to qualify for the paperback production line in a commercial library bindery.
  - A paperback with very narrow inner margins.
  - A paperback with fragile or brittle paper.
  - A paperback with text or other information on the inside of the front or back cover.

Causes
- Paper cover becomes soiled or worn and the text block damaged if the item does not have a protective cover.

Treatment
- Reinforce the paperback with a **pressboard** cover and a buckram spine.

Cost
- Batch production at approximately 5 minutes per item.
- Materials cost approximately 40 cents per item.

Equipment and Supplies
- Board shear
- Wrapped fire brick
- Scissors
- Ruler
- Glue brush
- Bone folder
- Sandpaper block
- Pressboard (pH neutral or alkaline, precut into standard paperback sizes)
- Buckram strips (precut 7 cm wide or purchased in precut rolls)
- Cambric hinge cloth, precut 2.5 cm wide
- Polyvinyl acetate (PVA) adhesive (dilute 2:1, PVA:water)
- Wastepaper
- Waxed paper

Operating Procedures—Typical Sequence
1. Select a paperback for pressboard reinforcement (photo 1).
2. Cut two pieces of pressboard for the cover boards, two strips of cambric for hinges and one strip of buckram for the spine, all to the exact height of the paperback. The width of the pressboard covers should be 6 mm narrower than the width of the paperback (photo 2). The grain of the pressboard must run parallel with the spine of the paperback or the boards will warp.
3. Apply glue to one of the cambric strips (photo 3).
4. Attach one-third of the width of the cambric strip to the spine edge of the paperback and fold the strip to make the hinge, leaving the glued side up (photo 4).
5. Position the cover board on the cambric hinge, exactly lining up the fore-edge of the cover with the fore-edge of the paperback. This will result in a 6-mm hinge (photo 5). Repeat steps 3 through 5 for the back cover.
6. Apply glue to the spine of the paperback and center it on the buckram strip (photo 6).
7. Apply glue to one side of the buckram strip and fold it over the cover. Bone in the hinge. Repeat for the other side (photo 7).

8. Place waxed paper inside the cover between the pressboard and the original paperback cover and weight until dry (photo 8).

Special Instructions

- To save time, batch paperbacks in groups of five.
- A typed label may be applied to the cover.
- If the original cover is glossy, lightly sand the spine and the hinge area where cambric and bookcloth will be attached.
- This procedure may not be appropriate for thick paperbacks, as the spine tends to become concave with use.
- This procedure is particularly useful for materials that must be put into immediate use, such as those for a reserve reading room. However, the reinforcement is only as *durable* as the attachment of the paper cover to the text block. If the leaves of the paperback were bound using an impermanent **hot melt adhesive,** the pressboard reinforcement will not prevent the leaves from detaching as the adhesive deteriorates.

PRESSBOARD REINFORCEMENT OF PAPERBACKS

Illustrated

1—Select a paperback for pressboard reinforcement.

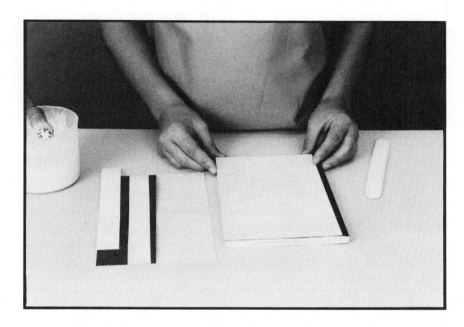

2—Cut materials for the pressboard reinforcement.

3—Apply glue to the cambric strip.

4—Attach the cambric hinge to the spine edge of the paperback.

5—Position the cover board on the cambric hinge.

6—Center the spine on the buckram strip.

7—Bone in the hinge of the cover.

8 — Weight the book until dry.

MENDING WITH JAPANESE PAPER AND STARCH PASTE

Problem
- Tears, voids, or weak folds in paper documents such as book pages, maps, and manuscripts.

Causes
- Normal wear and tear from frequent use, especially where paper has been folded and refolded.
- Rough or careless handling, especially around the edges.
- Weakened paper due to aging or exposure to deteriorative agents such as excessive heat or acidic materials.

Treatment
- Mend the tear or void with a water-torn strip of compatible Japanese paper applied with starch paste.

Cost
- Batch production at approximately 5 minutes per mend.
- Materials cost negligible per mend.

Equipment and Supplies
- Board shear
- Steel straightedge
- Scissors, embroidery or surgical
- Scalpel
- Japanese watercolor brush
- Bone folder
- Glue brush
- Japanese paper, assortment of thicknesses and shades, i.e., Sekishu white and natural, Goyu, Hosho, Tengujo, Kizukishi, Ginpai, Shoji
- Spatula
- Starch paste, wheat or rice
- Tiny whisk for mixing paste
- Blotting paper, white
- Pieces of glass for weights
- Light weights
- Wastepaper

Operating Procedures – Typical Sequence
1. Select an item for mending when the tear will worsen as the item is used.
2. Select a Japanese paper that is compatible with the item, i.e., similar color and thickness (photo 1). The mending paper should be slightly thinner than the item to be mended, to reduce stress on the mended edge.
3. Using the "water-tear" method, prepare a mending strip.
   a. Lay the straightedge on the sheet parallel with the **chain lines** and at a distance from the edge equal to the desired width of the mending strip.
   b. Using a Japanese watercolor brush, saturate the paper along the edge of the ruler. Take care to moisten evenly over a width of no more than 5 mm (photo 2).
   c. Bend the strip up against the straightedge and **crease** lightly with a bone folder (photo 3). Remove the straightedge and gently pull apart the fibers where they have been moistened and creased (photo 4). Repeat so that the strip has two soft, feathered edges. These edges help the mend blend into the item and prevent a hard line at the mend (photo 5).
4. Prepare wheat or rice starch paste according to the supplier's instructions.
5. Carefully align the beveled edges of the tear (photo 6).
6. Lay the mending strip on a piece of wastepaper and apply paste (photo 7). Care should be taken not to stretch the paper or the mend will **cockle** as it dries. The torn fibers should be

brushed out perpendicular to the strip. When repairing corner voids or edge tears, apply paste only to those areas of the mending strip that will overlap the item.

7. Lift the strip with a spatula (photo 8). Holding the ends loosely, position the strip over the tear (photo 9), and pat gently in place (photo 10).

8. Place the mended area between two pieces of blotting paper and dry under a light, even weight (photo 11). A long, narrow piece of plate glass should be used between the top blotter and the weight to distribute the weight evenly. Note that if too much paste has been used, the mend can stick to the blotting paper and removal may damage the item.

9. When the mend is completely dry, trim the excess mending strip with a small pair of scissors (photo 12) or a straightedge and scalpel.

Special Instructions

- Although there are other acceptable methods of mending tears (see "Mending with Heat-Set Tissue"), the use of pressure-sensitive tape is *not* acceptable. Many pressure-sensitive tapes deteriorate rapidly, stain paper, and are not easily removed. Tape should *never* be used on materials that will be kept for more than a year or two.

- For thin items likely to cockle, apply paste to a piece of glass and lightly drop the mending strip onto the pasted area. This will leave a very thin coat of paste on the strip.

- If there are numerous small tears or frayed edges on a document or map, it may be advisable to encapsulate the item in a polyester film envelope rather than attempting to mend every tear (see "Polyester Film Encapsulation").

- If a tear is curved, slightly overlap short mending strips along the curve of the tear.

- Plate glass used alone is a suitable weight for very small tears. Light weights can also be made from pieces of bookboard glued together and covered with bookcloth.

- Every tear has beveled edges that should be overlapped correctly when the tear is mended. If the paper was originally very strong and long-fibered, it may be possible to mend the tear by applying starch paste *very* sparingly with a microspatula to each beveled edge, pressing the tear together and drying between blotters. However, the page will never be as strong as it was before being torn.

MENDING WITH JAPANESE PAPER AND STARCH PASTE

Illustrated

1—Select a compatible Japanese paper to use for mending.

2—Saturate the paper along the edge of the straightedge.

3—Crease the strip lightly with a bone folder.

4—Gently pull the fibers apart where they have been moistened.

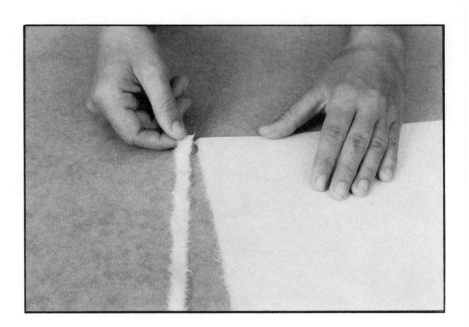

5—A fibered edge prevents a hard line at the edge of the mend.

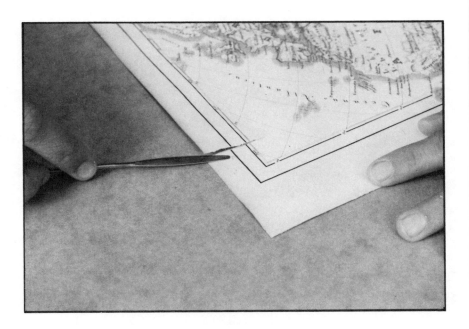

6—Carefully align the beveled edge of the tear.

7 — Apply paste to the mending strip.

8 — Lift the mending strip with a spatula.

9 — Position the strip over the tear.

10 — Pat gently in place.

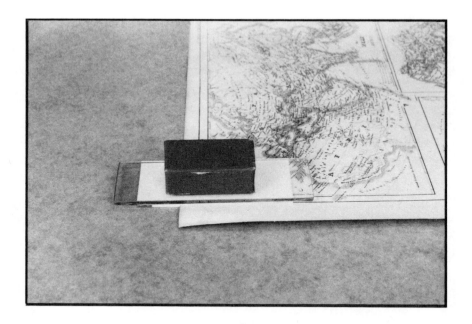

11 — Place the mended area between two pieces of blotting paper and under a light weight.

12 — Trim the excess mending strip.

MENDING WITH HEAT-SET TISSUE

Problem
- Tears or weak areas on coated paper.

Causes
- Normal wear and tear from frequent use, especially folding and unfolding.
- Rough or careless handling.

Treatment
- Mend the tear or weakened area with heat-set tissue.

Cost
- Batch production at approximately 5 minutes per mend.
- Materials cost negligible per mend.

Equipment and Supplies
- Scissors, small
- Pencil
- Magic Rub® eraser
- Heat-set tissue
- Remay® (non-woven polyester) or silicon release paper
- Tacking iron

Operating Procedures—Typical Sequence
1. Select an item for mending with heat-set tissue when the paper is coated (slick and shiny) (photo 1).
2. Place heat-set tissue over the tear or weakened area, shiny side down. On the dull side of the tissue, lightly pencil around the area to be mended, leaving no more than a 5-mm margin (photo 2).
3. Cut out the marked piece following the penciled line (photo 3). Gently erase pencil marks.
4. Lay the heat-set tissue over the area to be mended, *shiny side down.* Cover with a silicone or polyester release sheet. Apply light, even pressure to the tissue with preheated tacking iron set at medium heat (photo 4). Continue to apply light pressure until the mend becomes nearly invisible (photo 5).
5. If necessary, trim off excess tissue along the edge of the item.

Special Instructions
- The use of heat-set tissue for mending was greatly facilitated when the commercial firm Bookmakers began selling heat-set tissue made to the specifications of the Library of Congress Preservation Office.
- Heat-set tissue may be perforated with small, angled scalpel cuts and torn if a feathered edge is desired.
- Heat-set tissue can also be used to reinforce large areas which have been worn or weakened by very heavy use.
- Voids in a damaged item may be filled by using heat-set tissue on both sides of the item.
- If a chemical fume hood is available in the workshop, ethanol may be used sparingly to make the mend less visible and to facilitate adhesion. To use ethanol, lightly tack the heat-set tissue. Brush on a very small amount of ethanol and finish the tacking. A thin sheet of blotting paper should be used between the release sheet and the tacking iron to help absorb the ethanol vapor.

MENDING WITH HEAT-SET TISSUE

Illustrated

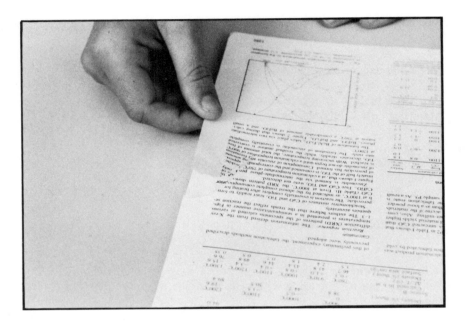

1 — Select an item for mending with heat-set tissue when the paper is coated.

2 — Lightly pencil on the tissue around the area to be mended.

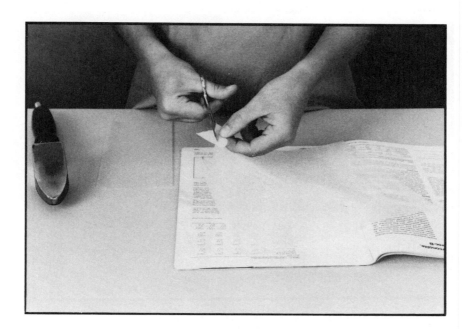

3 — Cut out the marked piece.

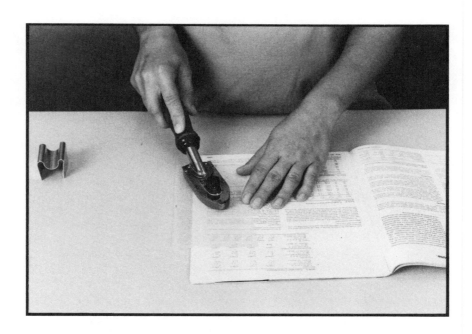

4 — Apply light, even pressure to the heat-set tissue with a tacking iron.

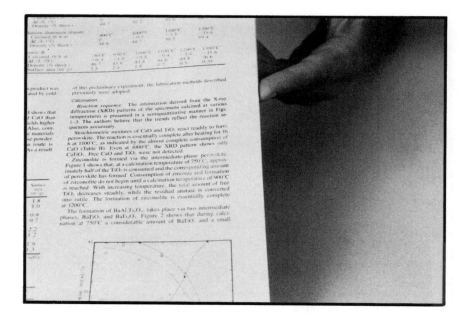

5— After continuous light pressure the mend becomes nearly invisible.

4
Protective Enclosure Procedures

POLYESTER FILM ENCAPSULATION

Problem
- Torn, damaged, or brittle paper document such as a manuscript, map, print, or poster, in need of overall physical protection.
- A paper document with many small edge tears too time-consuming to mend.
- A document which will receive heavy use.

Causes
- Paper which is fragile or brittle because of aging, acid deterioration, or exposure to excessive heat or atmospheric pollutants.
- Normal wear and tear from frequent use.
- Improper storage or abuse such as rolling or folding.

Treatment
- Encapsulate the document between two sheets of inert, transparent polyester film:
  - Remove surface dirt prior to encapsulation.
  - Hold film edges together with strips of double-sided pressure-sensitive tape so that the tape does not touch the document.

Cost
- Batch production at approximately 8 minutes per item.
- Materials cost approximately 60 cents per square foot.

Equipment and Supplies
- Board shear
- Corner rounder with 1/8-inch cutting blade
- Scissors, embroidery or surgical
- Shears, large
- Squeegee
- Large piece of glass
- One-Wipe® dust cloth
- Magic Rub® eraser
- Japanese utility brush or draftsman's dusting brush
- Polyester film; 2 mil, 3 mil, 4 mil, 5 mil; ICI Melinex® 516, Dupont Mylar® Type D, or 3M Scotchpar®.
- Double-sided tape, 3M Scotch Brand®, No. 415
- Weight, paperweight or small lead weight.
- Blotting paper, white

Operating Procedures—Typical Sequence
1. Select a document or map that needs complete physical protection because it is fragile, brittle, has many tears, or is subject to heavy use.
2. Place the item on a blotter and remove loose surface dirt by gently wiping the front and back of the item with a One-Wipe® dust cloth (photo 1).

3. Use a Magic Rub® eraser on smudges and very dirty areas, working lightly and carefully in a circular motion (photo 2). The purpose is to remove only *surface* dirt. Be careful not to abrade the paper. Sweep crumbs away with a Japanese utility brush or draftsman's dusting brush (photo 3).
4. Cut two sheets of polyester film at least 2.5 cm longer and wider than the item (photo 4).
5. Place one sheet of film on a large piece of glass and wipe over it with a One-Wipe® dust cloth. This will help the film adhere to the glass by developing a static charge.
6. Place the item to be encapsulated on the film and weight it down in the center.
7. Frame the item with strips of double-sided tape (photo 5). The tape should be placed 3 mm from the item. Leave very small gaps at the corners.
8. Place the second sheet of film over the item and weight the sandwich in the center.
9. Remove the paper backing from the tape on two perpendicular sides of the frame (photo 6). Using the squeegee and working diagonally away from the taped corner, force the air out of the sandwich (photo 7).
10. Remove the paper backing from the tape on the other two sides and squeegee again to seal the envelope on all four sides.
11. Trim the envelope on the board shear leaving a 1- to 3-mm border around the tape (photo 8).
12. Round the corners of the envelope on the corner rounder.

Special Instructions

*   Polyester encapsulation should not be used unless there is a specific reason to do so, such as extreme fragility or expected heavy use. Large quantities of film can add considerable bulk to a collection, and the glossy appearance of the film is objectionable to many researchers.
*   Unlike lamination, encapsulation is completely reversible. If necessary, the document can be removed quickly and easily from the film sandwich.
*   It is always advisable to deacidify acid paper *before* it is encapsulated. If the item is not deacidified, an alkaline sheet of paper should be encapsulated with the item when possible.
*   Polyester film is sold in rolls of various widths or in precut sheets. Precut sheets are convenient for encapsulating most items, especially standard-size documents. The thickness of the film to be used depends on the size and thickness of the item to be encapsulated.
*   ICI Melinex® 516, Dupont Mylar® Type D, and 3M Scotchpar® have been tested and are suitable for conservation use. Other films may not be suitable. Because polyester film is used for many different commercial applications, ordering instructions should clearly specify film type and physical qualities required. However, since manufacturers may change their product without notice, it is *safest* to order from a conservation supplier rather than direct from the manufacturer.
*   Because of the development of static charge on the film, polyester encapsulation is *not suitable* for pencil, pastel, or charcoal drawings or other items with flaking layers.

POLYESTER FILM ENCAPSULATION

Illustrated

1 — Remove loose surface dirt with a One Wipe® dust cloth.

2 — Use a Magic Rub® eraser on smudges and very dirty areas.

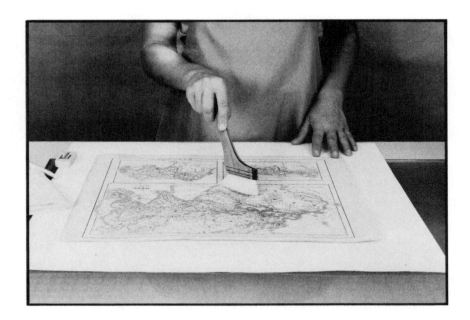

3—Remove eraser crumbs with a soft brush.

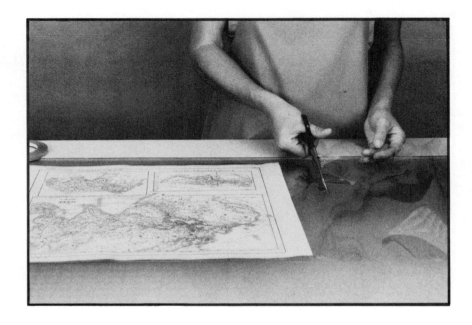

4—Cut two sheets of polyester film.

5—Frame the item with strips of double-sided tape.

6— Remove the paper backing from the tape on two perpendicular sides of the frame.

7 — Use a squeegee to force air out of the sandwich.

8 — Trim the envelope.

SIMPLE PORTFOLIO

Problem
- Physical protection needed for a thin item unsuitable for binding or rebinding because of age, format, paper condition, value, or projected use.
- Physical protection needed for unbound retrospective material that is infrequently used.

Causes
- Normal wear and tear from use or storage.
- Deteriorated condition caused by acid content of the paper or binding materials, or exposure to elevated temperatures or atmospheric pollutants.
- Thin item with an unusual format or historic interest unsuited to binding or rebinding.

Treatment
- Enclose the item in a portfolio of simple design.

Cost
- Batch production at approximately 20 minutes per item.
- Materials cost approximately 75 cents per item.

Equipment and Supplies
- Board shear
- Corner rounder
- Scissors
- Bone folder
- Cork-backed metal ruler
- Glue brush
- Boxboard or matboard, alkaline
- Map folder stock, alkaline (.010 or .020)
- Buckram, starch-filled in assorted colors
- Polyvinyl acetate (PVA) adhesive (dilute 3:1, PVA:water)
- Wrapped fire brick
- Wastepaper
- Waxed paper

Operating Procedures—Typical Sequence
1. Select an item for a portfolio when it is in fragile condition or when a hard-cover binding is inappropriate or inadvisable (photo 1). The item should not be over 2 cm thick.
2. Cut materials for a three-flap inner folder:
   a. To construct the fore-edge **flap**, cut a piece of map folder **stock** the length of the item by the **width** plus the **depth** (thickness) plus 2 cm (photo 2). (The additional 2 cm will serve as a tab for gluing.)
   b. To construct head and tail flaps, cut a piece of map folder stock the width of the item by two and a half times its length.
3. Mark flap pieces for folding:
   a. Fore-edge flap: mark the piece the exact width and the exact depth of the item.
   b. Head and tail flaps: center the item on the strip and mark its length at the head and tail, followed by its exact depth (photo 3).
4. Crease the folds over the cutting edge of the board shear:
   a. Leaving the blade up, clamp the flap piece so that the fold marks are lined up at the cutting edge of the board shear.
   b. Crease the fold by running a bone folder along the edge (photo 4). Repeat this step for all six folds.
5. Round the corners of the flaps (photo 5).
6. Trim the corners of the 2-cm tab on the fore-edge piece (photo 6).
7. Apply glue to the tab and attach it to the underside of the center section of the head and tail flap piece (photo 7).

8. Cut two cover boards the length of the item plus 6 mm by the width plus 3 mm. The grain of the board should run parallel to the length of the cover.

9. Cut two spine strips of buckram 8 cm wide, one the length of the item and one 4 cm longer (photo 8).

10. Glue the cover boards to the longer buckram strip (outer spine strip), leaving a space between the two boards equal to the depth of the item plus 6 mm to accommodate the added thicknesses of board, map folder stock, and buckram (photo 9). Apply glue, turn in and bone the head and tail of the spine strip.

11. Apply glue to inner spine strip and position it on the inside of the cover, taking care to bone in the joints (photo 10).

12. Apply glue to the back of the center section of the three-flap inner folder (photo 11).

13. Position the folder on the back cover board, with its open side lined up with the spine joint (photo 12). Open the flaps, place waxed paper on top of the glued area, and weight until dry (photo 13).

14. Attach a typed label to the front cover (photo 14).

Special Instructions

- Simple portfolios are typically constructed from scrap materials left over from other conservation procedures.

- There are many designs for simple portfolios that help protect items from mechanical damage. Libraries frequently share designs which can then be adapted to the needs of a particular collection. In addition, several commercial firms offer adjustable portfolios for thin items. While not very durable, these portfolios may be acceptable for little-used materials or a noncirculating collection.

SIMPLE PORTFOLIO

Illustrated

1 — Select a thin item for a simple portfolio when binding is inappropriate.

2 — Cut a piece of map folder stock for the fore-edge flap.

3 — Mark for folds at the head and tail.

4 — Crease folds over the edge of the board shear.

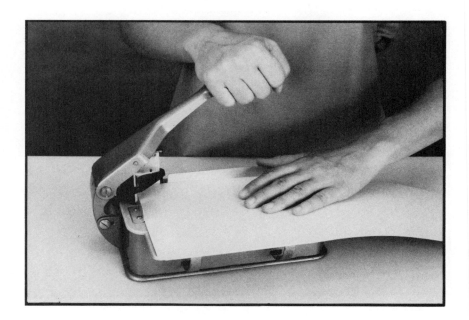

5—Round the corners of the flaps.

6—Trim the corners of the tab.

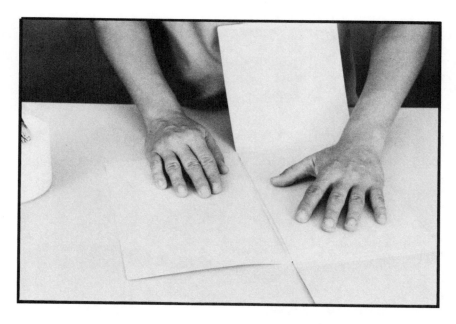

7—Glue the tab to the underside of the center section.

8—Cut materials for the cover of the portfolio.

9—Glue the cover boards to the spine strip.

10—Bone the inner spine strip in place.

11 — Apply glue to the back of the center section of the three-flap folder.

12 — Position the folder on the back cover board.

13—Place waxed paper on top of the glued area and weight until dry.

14—Attach a typed label to the front cover.

PHASE BOX

Problem
- Damaged or deteriorated book that will suffer further mechanical damage if left unprotected; or a book with a loose or detached cover, loose or detached leaves, or brittle paper.
- Physical protection needed for an item that will eventually be replaced, reformatted, or given full conservation treatment.
- Infrequently used item in disrepair.
- Group of unbound materials, such as retrospective issues of a periodical, which need protection but are unsuitable for binding.
- Fragile item requested for circulation or interlibrary loan.
- A damaged book that is large or heavy for which repair or rebinding is not feasible at the present time.
- A book with a damaged binding that does not warrant the expense of a double-tray box or full conservation treatment.

Causes
- Deterioration from use or abuse over the years, including storage in a damaging environment, improper shelving practices, or rough or careless handling.
- Breakdown of the binding structure due to deterioration or aging of component materials such as glue, thread, paper, cloth, leather, etc.
- Damaged binding due to inadequate original binding, previous improper repair, or deliberate mutilation.
- Materials which have been left unbound.

Treatment
- Enclose the item in portfolio made from durable boxboard. The portfolio is custom-made so that the item is held snugly inside. The construction procedure is simple and easily adapted to mass production.

Cost
- Batch production at approximately 30 minutes per box.
- Materials cost approximately $1.00 per box.

Equipment and Supplies
- Board shear
- "Phase Box Maker" (crimping machine for boxboard)
- Measurephase® (phase box measuring device)
- Corner rounder
- **Rivet** fastening machine
- Boxboard, alkaline/lignin-free (.060)
- Matboard, museum quality
- Polyvinyl acetate (PVA) adhesive (dilute 3:1, PVA:water)
- Awl
- Braided nylon cord or waxed linen thread
- Polyethylene washers, 2-cm diameter with a 3-mm diameter center hole
- Rivets, two-part, 1/8 inch
- Magic Rub® eraser
- Labels to read "fold this flap first"

Operating Procedures—Typical Sequence
1. Measure and record the length (l), width (w), and depth (d) of the item using a phase box measuring device or a triangle and ruler (photo 1).
2. On the board shear, cut horizontal and vertical strips of boxboard (photo 2). The grain direction of the board should run parallel with the *short* dimension of the strip (fig. 4.1).

a.   The width of the horizontal strip is equal to the length of the item plus 3 mm. The length of the strip is equal to three times the depth of the item plus three times the width plus 3 cm.

b.   The width of the vertical strip equals the width of the item. The length of the strip equals two and a half times the length of the item plus two times the depth plus 1.2 cm.

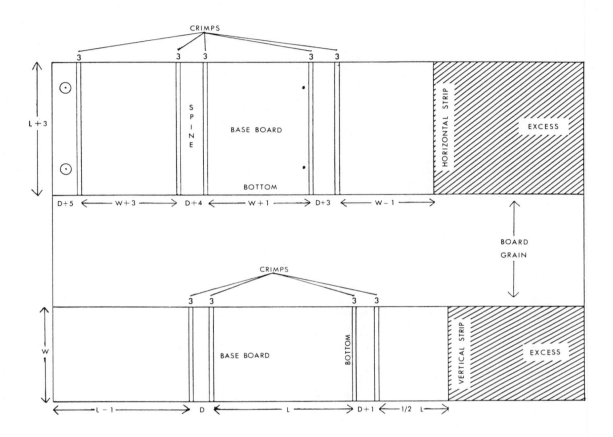

Fig. 4.1. Diagram for a phase box.

3.   Along one side of each strip, measure and mark for **crimps,** adding and subtracting from the recorded dimensions as shown in figure 4.1 (photo 3).

4.   Round the corners of the strips on a corner rounder.

5.   Center the crimp marks under the crimping blade of the Phase Box Maker and crimp the strips to allow folding of the boxboard (photo 4).

6.   Erase the pencil marks from the strips with a Magic Rub® eraser.

7.   Mark the position of holes for ties on the outside of the fore-edge side of the base of the horizontal strip (figure 4.1) (photo 5).

8.   Punch holes for ties with an awl (photo 6).

9.   String thread through the holes from the inside out (photo 7). Pull the thread taut on the inside and smooth with a bone folder.

10.   Mark the placement of washers slightly to the inside of the string when it is pulled up over the fore-edge of the box (photo 8). Punch holes through the marks with an awl.

11. Using the rivet-setting machine, attach the washers to the fore-edge flap (photo 9).
12. Apply glue to the outside of the **baseboard** of the vertical strip (photo 10) and position on the inside of the baseboard of the horizontal strip (fig. 4.2).

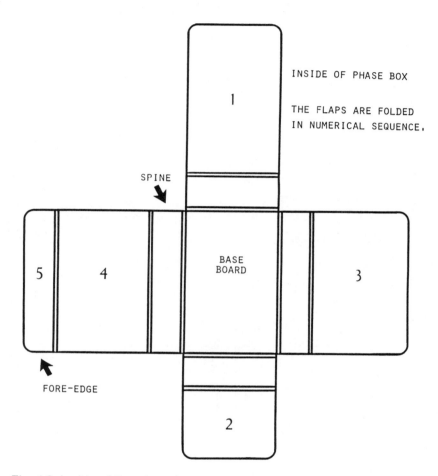

Fig. 4.2. Inside of the phase box.

13. Weight the glued area until dry (photo 11).
14. Attach a "fold this flap first" label to the inside of flap 1 (figure 4.2). If desired, the flaps may be numbered to assist the user in closing the box.
15. Close the phase box and secure it by winding the thread around the washers (photo 12). Knot the ends of the thread to prevent unraveling.
16. Type a label on scrap endsheet paper and attach to the spine.

Special Instructions

- Labels should be typed with a carbon, non-correctable film ribbon. If a carbon ribbon is not available, the label should be photocopied onto alkaline paper. Spraying the label with Krylon®, a plastic fixative, will help keep the label clean.
- Phase box making is most efficient when performed in large batches. Measurements can be reduced to simple formulas so that cutting and assembly steps can be performed for a large number of items at one time. However, it is also desirable to organize workflow so that

phase boxes can be constructed on a "rush" basis for fragile items that are going to circulate out of the building.
- A number of commercial firms supply custom-made phase boxes from customer measurements. Individual libraries may wish to explore this alternative and compare costs.

PHASE BOX

Illustrated

1—Measure and record the dimensions of the item.

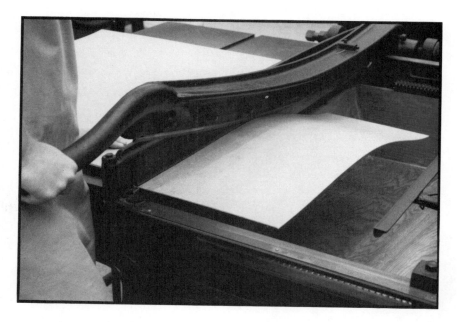

2—Cut horizontal and vertical strips.

3—Mark the strips for crimping.

4 — Crimp the strips to allow folding of the boxboard.

5 — Mark the position of the holes for ties.

6—Punch holes for ties with an awl.

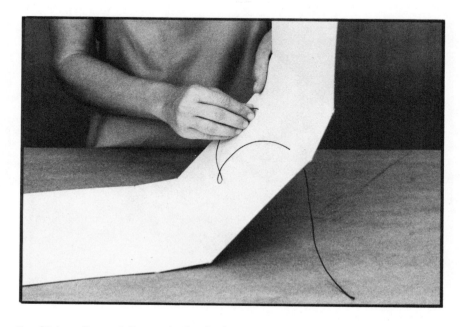

7—String thread through the holes.

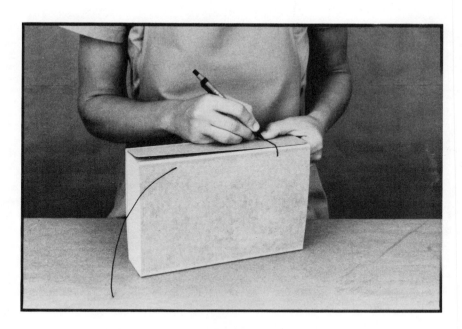

8—Mark for placement of washers.

9—Rivet the washers to the fore-edge flap.

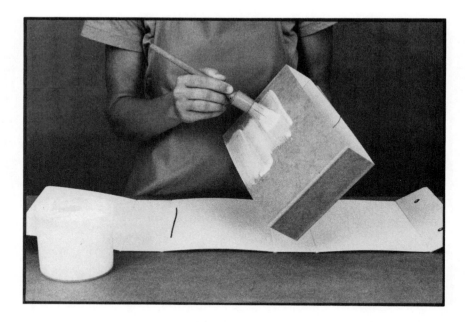

10—Apply glue to the baseboard of the vertical strip.

11—Weight the glued area until dry.

12—Secure the phase box by winding the ties around the washers.

DOUBLE-TRAY BOX

Problem
- Damaged or deteriorated book for which rebinding or full conservation treatment is inappropriate or unfeasible.
- Rare or valuable book which would benefit from additional protection.
- Unbound item or group of prints or manuscripts for which binding is inappropriate.
- Fragile or vulnerable binding that would sustain physical or mechanical damage if left unprotected, including books with elaborate gold tooling or an unusual format.

Causes
- Breakdown of the binding structure due to deterioration or aging of component materials, especially the acid-deterioration of vegetable-tanned leather.
- Damage to the binding from exposure to excessive heat, ultraviolet light rays, dirt, dust, and atmospheric pollutants such as sulfur dioxide and ozone.
- Damaged binding due to inadequate original binding, especially overpared leather in the hinge area and weak attachment of the cover boards.

Treatment
- Enclose the item in a box made from alkaline binder's board covered in buckram and lined with alkaline paper:
  - The box should fit the item exactly and permit easy removal.
  - The box acts as a buffer against fluctuations in temperature and humidity, and protects from dust, light, atmospheric pollutants, abrasion, and mechanical damage.

Cost
- Batch production at approximately 1½ hours per box.
- Materials cost approximately $3.00 per box.

Equipment and Supplies
- Board shear
- Stamping press, type, type cabinet, rubber-tipped electrician's clamps, tweezers, stamping foil
- Cork-backed metal ruler
- Triangle
- Glue brushes
- Scissors, embroidery or surgical
- Shears
- Scalpel
- Spatula
- Wrapped lead weights
- Bookboard, "Acid-pHree" Davey Red Label®, caliper .082
- Buckram, starch-filled in assorted colors
- Lining (endsheet) paper, alkaline
- Polyvinyl acetate (PVA) adhesive (dilute 3:1, PVA:water)
- Starch paste, wheat or rice
- Soft cloth
- Wastepaper
- Waxed paper

Operating Procedures — Typical Sequence
1. Measure the length (l), depth (d), and width (w) of the book (photos 1-3) and record the measurements on the Calculation Form for Box Components (fig. 4.3).

```
                Inside Tray                          Outside Tray                        Cover

Book            2 sides    fore-edge base            2 sides    fore-edge      base       2 covers  spine

L____ + 6mm              = Lf____ = Lb____ + 7mm              = Lf____       = Lb____ + 5mm = Lc____   = Lsp____
W____ + 1mm = Ws____              + 3mm = Wb____ + 3mm = Ws____       + 2mm = Wb____ + 3mm = Wc____
D____ + 1mm = Ds____     = Df____        + 4mm = Ds____ = Df____             + 3mm         = Dsp____
```

Fig. 4.3. Calculation Form for Box Components.

2. Calculate the dimensions of the box pieces by filling in the form.
3. Select a piece of bookboard and, following the form, cut pieces for the *inside tray* (two sides, one fore-edge, and one base piece); *outside tray* (2 sides, one fore-edge, and one base piece); and *cover* (two cover boards and one spine piece) (photo 4) (fig. 4.4) All pieces, except the side pieces, should be cut with the grain direction of the board parallel with the spine of the box.

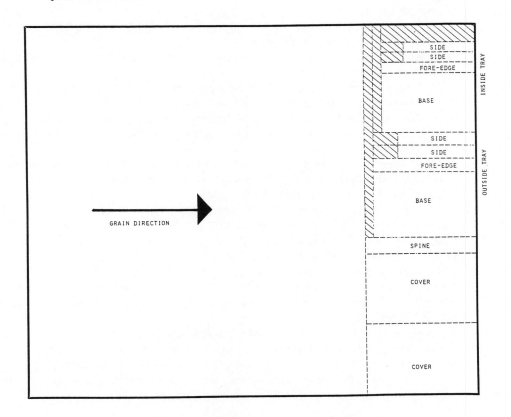

Fig. 4.4. Cut bookboard pieces for the double-tray box.

4. Assemble the inside tray.
   a. Using a small glue brush, apply glue to the bottom edge of the fore-edge piece (photo 5).
   b. Position the fore-edge piece on the baseboard and brace it with lead weights so that it is perpendicular to the base (photo 6).
   c. Apply glue to the bottom and one edge of a side piece and position it on the base board at a right angle to the fore-edge piece (photo 7).
   d. Repeat for the other side piece and brace the tray, weighting the corners (photo 8).

5. Repeat step 4 for the outside tray. Allow the trays to dry thoroughly. The outside tray should fit exactly without being tight over the inside tray (photo 9).
6. Cut buckram strips to cover the sides of the trays (photo 10). The grain direction of the cloth (as indicated by the selvage edge) should run the length of the sides. Each strip is equal to twice the length of the sides plus the length of the fore-edge plus 3 cm for turn-ins. The strip is cut wide enough to cover both sides of the tray wall plus 3 cm for turn-ins.
7. Apply glue to the outside of one tray side and position it on the wrong side of the buckram strip, leaving a turn-in allowance of 1.5 cm on the end and bottom of the base (photo 11). Smooth the buckram and use a bone folder to ensure adhesion. Apply glue to the outside of the fore-edge side (photo 12), turn the tray, and place the side on the buckram, keeping the cloth taut as the tray is turned (photo 13). Glue and attach the remaining side (photo 14).
8. Clip the buckram at the corners of the bottom of the base (photo 15). Make further cuts and clips at the corners in preparation for covering the inside tray walls (photos 16-19).
9. Apply glue and turn in the buckram on the sides and bottom of the tray as illustrated in photos 20-24. Carefully bone in joints and corners.
10. Repeat steps 7-9 for outside tray.
11. Construct the box cover.
    a. Cut a rectangle of buckram for the cover, allowing 2 cm turn-ins and hinges equal to twice the thickness of the boards.
    b. Attach the spine piece to the buckram and stamp author and title. (See steps 9-12 of "New Cover.")
    c. Attach the cover boards to the buckram (photo 25), trim the corners, and turn excess buckram onto the cover boards (photo 26).
    d. Cut a strip of buckram equal to the length of the inside tray by the width of the spine plus 5 cm. Attach the strip to the inside of the spine (photo 27) and bone in the joint (photo 28).
12. Cut two sheets of alkaline paper to line the trays; each sheet is 2 mm less than the length and 2 cm wider than the inside dimensions of the corresponding tray (photo 29). The grain of the paper should run parallel to the spine.
13. Apply paste to the paper, brushing in the direction of the grain (photo 30). Allow the **paper fibers** to relax, i.e., the paper loses its curl and becomes limp. Holding the paper by opposite corners, lower it into the tray and rub in place with a soft cloth (photo 31). Turn the excess paper onto the bottom of the tray.
14. Lay the box cover face down, making sure the stamping is not upside down! Apply a generous amount of glue to the bottom of the outside tray (photo 32) and position it on the left side of the cover. Line up the open edge of the tray *exactly* with the edge of the cover board (photo 33).
15. Test the position of the inside tray by holding it against the right side of the cover while holding the glued outside tray securely in place (photo 34). Glue the inside tray in place.
16. Weight the trays with lead weights, especially the corners and edges (photo 35).
17. The book should fit exactly in the inside tray without rubbing against the tray sides (photo 36). The covered trays should fit snugly together (photo 37).

Special Instructions

- Custom-made boxes are available from individuals and commercial firms. Accurate measurements are essential for construction of a properly fitting box when the maker does not have the book in hand.
- **Pryroxlin-coated buckram** and bookcloth are durable covering material, but not suitable for use on trays. A combination of a buckram cover with contrasting bookcloth or marbled paper sides makes an attractive box. A leather label on the spine adds distinction to a box.
- When there are slight variations in the size of individual volumes of a set, the trays should

be made to fit each volume exactly, but the covers should be made a uniform height. The printing on the spines should also be uniform.

- If the trays are lined with paper and allowed to dry completely before being attached to the cover, the box will warp. It is best to line the trays immediately before they are attached to the cover.
- Double-tray boxes for most books can be constructed from .082 bookboard. If appropriate, another thickness of board can be used. However, the measurement form in figure 4.3 would have to be adjusted accordingly. Formulas may also need to be adjusted for different covering materials.
- Some books, particularly very valuable books or books with structural peculiarities, may warrant construction of special boxes with special features.

DOUBLE-TRAY BOX

Illustrated

1—Measure the length (l) of the book.

2—Measure the depth (d) of the book.

3—Measure the width (w) of the book.

4—Cut the box pieces.

5—Apply glue to the bottom edge of the fore-edge piece.

6—Position the fore-edge piece on the base board.

7— Position the side piece on the base board at a right angle to the fore-edge piece.

8 — Brace all three sides of the tray and weight the corners.

9 — The outside tray should fit exactly over the inside tray without being tight.

10—Cut buckram strips to cover the sides of the trays.

11—Position the side of the tray on the buckram strip.

12—Apply glue to the fore-edge sides.

13—Keep the cloth taut as the tray is turned.

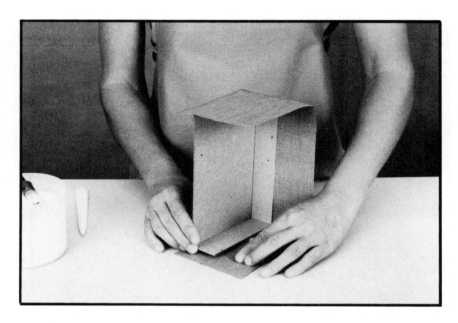

14 — Glue and attach the remaining side.

15 — Clip the buckram at the corners.

16 — Clip no. 1.

17 — Clip no. 2.

18—Clip no. 3.

19—Clip no. 4.

20 — The cloth on the bottom of the tray is turned in.

21 — Tabs cover the inside corners.

22—The large tab covers the edge of the tray side.

23—Apply glue and turn in the cloth on the inside of the tray side.

24 — Turn in the cloth on the inside of the tray fore-edge.

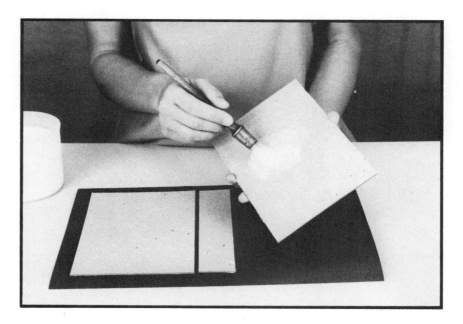

25 — Attach the cover boards to the buckram.

26—Turn the excess cloth onto the cover boards.

27—Attach a buckram strip inside of the cover spine.

28 — Bone securely in the joints.

29 — Cut paper to line the trays.

30 — Apply paste, brushing with the grain of the paper.

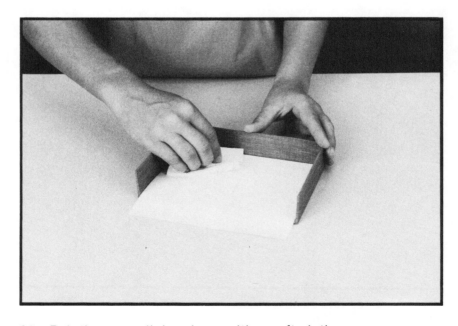

31 — Rub the paper lining down with a soft cloth.

32 — Apply glue to the tray bottom.

33 — Line up the open edge of the outside tray exactly with the edge of the cover board.

34—Test the position of the inside tray.

35—Weight the trays.

36 — The book should fit exactly without rubbing against the tray sides.

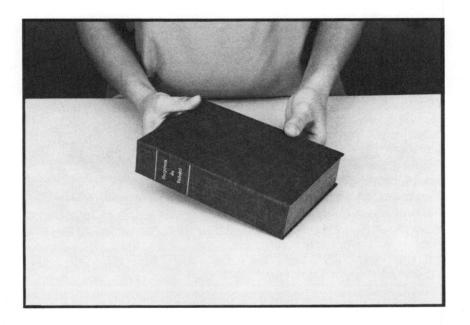

37 — The covered outside tray fits snugly over the inside tray.

POLYESTER BOOK

Problem • Seriously deteriorated book with fragile or brittle paper.
—The book cannot be used in its present format without further damage or possible loss of text.
—The book contains illustrations or has a large format not satisfactorily preserved by photoreproduction.
—It is desirable to retain the original leaves for their research or artifactual value.

Causes • Deteriorated component materials, especially paper, due to acid content, improper storage conditions, and atmospheric pollutants.

Treatment • Disbind the book and separate the text block into individual **leaves**; remove surface dirt, selectively mend, deacidify, and encapsulate each leaf; and rebind the encapsulated leaves.

Cost • Time is dependent on the size and number of leaves; approximately 3 minutes per leaf.
• Materials cost approximately 50 cents per leaf plus $1.00.

Equipment and Materials
• Ultrasonic Welder for Polyester Film Encapsulation
• Wei T'o Soft Spray® (non-aqueous deacidification system)
• Velo-bind® Machine (paper punch)
• Board shear
• Book press
• Metal-edged pressing boards
• Corner rounder with 1/8-inch cutting blade
• Steel straightedge
• Self-centering triangle
• Bone folder
• Scalpel
• Tiny whisk
• Spatula
• Japanese utility brush or draftsman's dusting brush
• One Wipe® dust cloth
• Magic Rub® eraser
• Blotting paper, white
• Japanese water color brush
• Japanese paper
• Starch paste, wheat or rice
• Polyester film, precut sheets, 2 mil, 3 mil; ICI Melinex 516®, Dupont Mylar® Type D, 3-M Scotchpar®
• Endsheet paper, alkaline
• Bristol, caliper .010, .020
• Bookboard, "Acid-pHree" Davey Red Label®, caliper .060, .082, .090
• Buckram, starch-filled
• Super cloth
• Unbleached linen thread
• Polyvinyl acetate (PVA) adhesive (dilute 2:1, PVA:water)
• Mixture of PVA and starch paste, 1:3
• Waxed paper
• Wastepaper

Operating Procedures—Typical Sequence

1. Select a book for rebinding into a polyester book format when the paper is too brittle for conventional rebinding and the book is unusable in its present condition (photo 1).
2. Disbind and separate the text block into individual leaves (photo 2). Trim each leaf to approximately the same size but trim as *little as possible,* removing just enough to leave an even edge.
3. Remove surface dirt from soiled pages. (See steps 2 and 3 of "Polyester Film Encapsulation.")
4. Deacidify each leaf using Wei T'o Soft Spray® system or another suitable deacidification method (photo 3).
5. *Selectively* mend large tears or voids. (See "Mending with Japanese Paper and Starch Paste" or "Mending with Heat-Set Tissue.")
6. Select precut sheets of polyester film the approximate size of the leaves.
   a. Trim a polyester bottom sheet for each leaf leaving at least a 6-mm margin on all four sides.
   b. Trim a top polyester sheet for each leaf leaving an inner margin of at least 5 cm for a hinge and at least a 6-mm margin on the remaining three sides.
7. Encapsulate each leaf using the Minter Ultrasonic Welder for Polyester Film Encapsulation (photo 4).
8. Trim the encapsulated leaves to *exactly* the same size, and round the fore-edge corners.
9. Prepare component materials for the binding. Cut to the same height as the encapsulated leaves: two endsheets the width of the sheets, two strips of buckram 7 cm wide, two pieces of super 5 cm wide, and several strips of bristol 7 mm wide (for fillers).
10. Using a Velo-bind machine, punch sewing holes in all components above except two of the bristol strips (photo 5). The Velo-bind machine gives an inner margin of 3 mm and places holes 2.5 cm apart. For a larger inner margin or differently spaced holes, see "Special Instructions" below.
11. Intersperse filler strips between the polyester sheets at the inner margin to build up the binding edge to the same thickness as the encapsulated leaves (photo 6).
12. Arrange the spine layers in order: super, buckram strip, endsheet, text (encapsulated leaves and fillers), endsheet, buckram strip, and super (photo 7). In preparation for sewing, line up the holes, and secure the whole sandwich with a bulldog clip.
13. Beginning at the center of the binding edge, side-sew the text block with heavy linen thread in a figure-eight fashion (photo 8). (See "Pamphlet Binding" for sewing instructions.)
14. Apply glue to a bristol strip and position it over the exposed stitching on the text block (photo 9). Bone down securely and repeat for the back of the text block.
15. Apply glue on top of the attached bristol strip and fold and bone the super back over it. Repeat for the back of the text block.
16. Apply glue to the top of the super and fold and bone the buckram back over it (photo 10). Repeat for the back of the text block.
17. Cut cover boards leaving a 3-mm square on the head, tail, and fore-edge and a 12-mm hinge area on the spine edge. (The width of the hinge is equal to twice the width of the filler strips.)
18. Prepare the cover boards for an inset front label.
    a. Prepare a stamped label or prepare the original label for reuse.
    b. Cut two pieces of heavy paper (100 pound) the same size as the cover boards and, using a self-centering triangle or ruler, measure for a cut-out the same size as the label (photo 11).
    c. Using a scalpel and a straight edge, remove the measured area from *one* piece of paper.
    d. Attach the paper with the window to the front cover board and attach the second piece of paper to the back cover board.
19. Cut a rectangle of buckram for the cover.

20. Cut a spine strip of bristol the height of the cover boards and the width of the spine (depth of sewn area).
21. Attach the spine strip and the cover boards to the covering material, making sure the board with the cut-out is in the proper position (photo 12). Flip the cover and *carefully* bone the edges of the inset (photo 13). Trim the corners of the buckram and turn in excess material onto the cover boards (photo 14).
22. Position the polyester text block on the cover and place a piece of wastepaper between the buckram hinge and the endsheet. Glue the super hinge to the buckram. Apply glue to the buckram hinge (photo 15), and pull out the wastepaper and replace with a piece of waxed paper. Carefully close the cover, holding the text block firmly in place (photo 16).
23. Bone in the outside hinge (photo 17). Repeat steps 22 and 23 for the back of the book.
24. Press the book between metal-edged boards in a book press until dry.
25. Cut two pieces of endsheet paper to fit on the inside of the covers leaving a 3-mm margin on all sides (the height should be the same as the text block). Brushing with the grain, apply mixture to the endsheet and attach it to the inside of the cover boards, front and back (photo 18).
26. Apply glue to the label and attach it to the front cover using a mixture of PVA and starch paste for a paper label or PVA alone for an original cloth label (photo 19). Smooth down the edges to ensure complete adhesion. Place a piece of blotting paper over the front cover and return the book to the press to dry.
27. The finished book should open easily, and the leaves should lie flat (photo 20).

Special Instructions

- Because each leaf will be encapsulated, not all tears need to be mended.
- For large items such as atlases, or where a Velo-bind machine is not available, a template can be made and a small hollow paper drill or punch used to make sewing holes.
- Depending on the item, a wider binding margin may be desirable. If so, adjust the width of fillers, bristol strips, gutter margin, etc.
- Fold-out maps or illustrations can be incorporated into a polyester book. However, because polyester does not fold easily, the map must be cut into sections and polyester cloth such as Remay® or Cerex® used as hinges. The decision to cut a map should be made in consultation with the custodial division responsible for the item.
- Recent studies at the Library of Congress, Preservation Research and Testing Office have determined that the less expensive and lighter-weight polypropylene film can be substituted for polyester film in the fabrication of polyester books.

POLYESTER BOOK

Illustrated

1 —Select a seriously deteriorated book with paper too brittle for conventional rebinding.

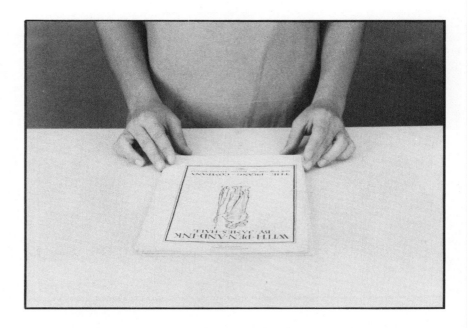

2—Disbind and separate the text block into individual leaves.

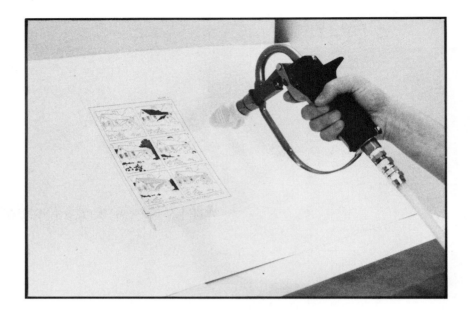

3 — Deacidify each leaf.

4 — Encapsulate each leaf leaving a hinge for binding.

5—Prepare binding components for the text block.

6 — Intersperse filler strips between the polyester hinges to build up the sewing edge.

7—Arrange the spine layers in order.

8—Side-sew the text block with a heavy linen thread.

9 — Attach a bristol strip over the exposed sewing.

10 — Fold the buckram strip over the glued super.

11—Measure for a cut-out the same size as the label.

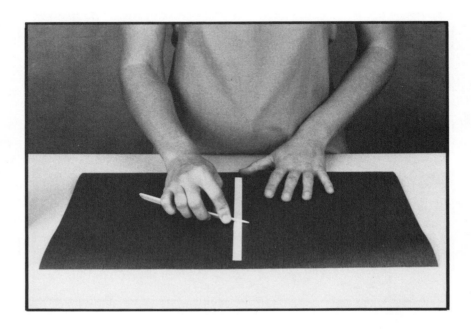

12—Attach the spine strip and the cover boards to the covering material.

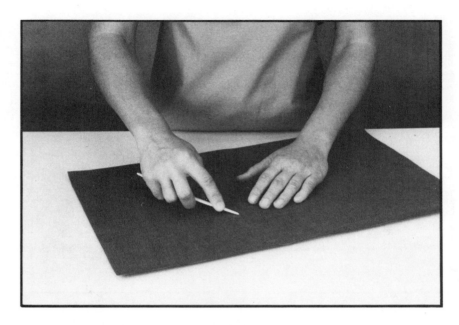

13 — Carefully bone the edges of the insert.

14 — Trim the corners of the covering material.

15—Position the text block in the cover and apply glue to the hinge.

16—Carefully close the cover, holding the text block in place.

17 — Bone in the hinge.

18 — Attach the endsheet to the inside of the cover board.

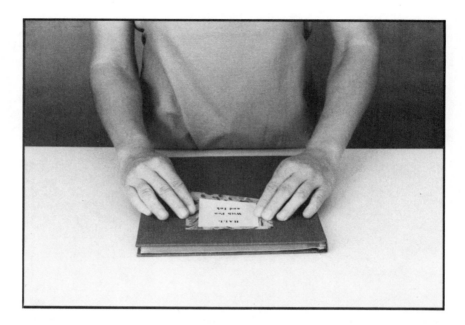

19—Attach the inlay label to the front cover.

20—The finished binding should open easily and lie flat.

Appendix 1
Decision-Making Checklist for Book Repair

The decision-making process for book repair involves asking questions that can be answered by examining the book. Most of these questions can be answered easily because most repair problems are routine and quickly identified. However, individual decisions are still made on the basis of expected use, book condition and structure, available options, and costs.

Seriously deteriorated items that cannot be easily repaired in-house should enter a different decision-making process. This category would include brittle books (paper suffering from acid deterioration), or books that would require hours of tedious repair or treatment. In addition, some items may need treatment that is beyond the expertise of local personnel. The issues of withdrawal, retention and extensive conservation treatment, or reformatting are collection development decisions more appropriately left to bibliographers, subject specialists, or collection development officers.

The following questions are representative of the decision-making process. In practice, the answers usually come automatically, and decisions can be made quickly and efficiently.

How Is the Book Constructed?

- Is the book small, average, or large? How will it be shelved? Is the text block thick or thin?
- What is the method of leaf attachment? Sewn-through-the-fold? Sewn over tapes? Adhesive-bound? Side-sewn? Oversewn?
- Is the page attachment intact, or is the text block broken apart or loose and separated in spots?
- Is the text block rounded or flat backed? Has the spine become concave or started to sag?
- How wide are the inner margins?
- Is the original binding on the book or has it been rebound?
- Has the book been previously mended? If so, with what materials? Are the mending materials permanent, or are they causing damage or stress to the structure of the book?

Is the Cover Protecting the Text Block?

- Is the text block loose in its case?
- Are the endsheets torn at the hinge?
- Is the super intact or is it torn?
- Have the endsheets or the super lifted away from the coverboards?
- Are the linings on the spine adequate? Are they deteriorated or detached?
- Is the cover material made of cloth, paper, leather, or a combination of materials? Is the cover soiled or torn? Is it seriously faded?
- Is the lettering on the spine legible? Is the call number legible?
- Are the hinges of the cover deteriorated or torn?
- Is the head or tail worn?
- Are the corners of the cover broken? Frayed? Worn and rounded?
- Has the cover been vandalized? Spilled on, dog-chewed, slashed, or soaked?

What Is the Condition of the Paper?

- Is the paper strong and flexible? Is it soft, pulpy, and weak? Is it brittle, e.g., does it break off when a corner is flexed?
- Is the paper coated so it's slick and glossy? Does the book contain plates printed on coated paper?
- Are there torn pages?
- Has the paper been mended with pressure-sensitive tape?
- Is there evidence of acid migration from the cover or endsheets onto the text block?

Does the Book Have an Unusual Format or Other Feature?

- Are the endsheets important to the content of the book (e.g., maps or illustrations)?
- Are there plates or maps? Are any missing? Are any loose?
- Are there missing or mutilated pages?
- Are there pages or plates that fold at the fore-edge? Are there maps that fold out?
- Is there pocket material?
- Are there loose errata slips?
- Have the bolts of the sections been cut?

How Will the Book Be Used?

- Will the book be heavily used? Will it be infrequently used?
- What is the subject of the book?
- What is the date of publication?
- Is it a reference book? How is it used?
- How often has the book circulated in the past year? The past five years?
- Are there other copies in the library? In what location?
- Are there newer or older editions of the work? Does the library own them?
- Has the book been reprinted?
- Will this edition be superseded? When?
- Is the book part of a multi-volume set? Have any of the other volumes been previously rebound or repaired?
- Is the book one volume of a serial publication? What is the condition of the rest of the holdings?

What Will It Cost to Repair the Book?

- Can the book be easily repaired?
- Does it need to be repaired quickly?
- How much time would it take to repair it? How much would the materials and labor cost?
- Who can do the work? How quickly can it be done?

Are There Other Options Besides Repair?

- Could the book be recased at a library bindery? Would that be cheaper or more appropriate than repairing the book in-house?
- Could the book be rebound at a library bindery? Hand-sewn through the fold? Oversewn? Adhesive-bound?
- Would a protective box or portfolio be more appropriate than repair?

Appendix 2
Developing In-House Capabilities: Profiles of Four Hypothetical Libraries

Libraries should develop the capability to perform only those procedures that match the needs of their collections, their ability to purchase equipment and supplies, and their available personnel. The following examples of four hypothetical libraries illustrate how a conservation strategy might be developed. It should be emphasized, however, that in-house conservation and maintenance activities, although vitally important, are only *one* aspect of a comprehensive preservation program. In addition to physical treatment, libraries should develop specific programs for environmental control, storage and handling, disaster preparedness, and staff and patron education. In-house treatment must also be closely coordinated with the library's commercial binding program and policies for the replacement or reformatting of seriously deteriorated items.

Library A

Library A is a medium-sized academic library with a relatively new collection housed in a modern, air-conditioned building. The library's major conservation needs are to repair books damaged through ordinary use, to repair heavily used reference and reserve materials, and to execute minor repairs on inadequate publisher's bindings. Library A has a modest amount of money to spend on supplies and equipment, one full-time paraprofessional responsible for both conservation work and for preparing journals for commercial library binding, and an ample budget for part-time student assistants. Given their modest needs, Library A should concentrate on the book repair procedures of "Tightening the Hinges of a Case-bound Book" and "Recasing Using the Original Cover." Rather than investing in bookcloth and buckram and over-burdening the small staff, items whose cloth cases need repair should be sent to the commercial library bindery, along with books in need of protective enclosure. However, the addition of supplies for "Paperback Reinforcement," "Pressboard Reinforcement of Paperbacks," and "Pamphlet Binding" would allow Library A to bind certain items inexpensively and efficiently in-house, thereby reserving the binding budget for rebinding and recasing. Likewise, paper mending procedures could be easily implemented, and the addition of supplies for "Polyester Film Encapsulation" would allow for the protection of heavily used maps. These latter procedures could be taught to student assistants assigned to public service areas. Because of the good condition of its collection and a favorable storage environment, Library A's conservation needs can be simply met if preventative measures are emphasized.

Library B

Library B is a small, specialized research library. Although connected with a large, prestigious university, Library B is privately endowed and fiscally and administratively separate from the university library. Since a carefully chosen private library forms the core of the collection, most of Library B's very valuable items are in good condition. Funds are allocated on a regular basis for extensive conservation treatment for valuable items by an experienced conservator in private practice. However, Library B also contains a high proportion of unstable, vulnerable, and fragile materials that do not have great *individual* value, but are important to the collection as a whole.

Under the direction of a curator, Library B could develop the capability for "Protective Enclosure Procedures" and "Mending with Japanese Paper and Starch Paste." Although Library B hopes to hire a full-time conservator in the future, for the time being a graduate assistant could be trained to execute these procedures. An active "friends" organization is eager to assist in simple conservation work. These volunteers could be organized by a curator and trained by a conservator/consultant who would hold a workshop demonstrating proper techniques. By concentrating on procedures that do not alter the physical item, Library B is ensuring that its conservation efforts are appropriate to a collection composed largely of items with intrinsic value.

Library C

Library C is a large university library, with a number of departmental libraries scattered around the campus, and a central collection housed in a cramped building that is not air-conditioned. By conservative estimate, 30 percent of the books in the central collection have deteriorated to the point where the paper can not be used without danger of loss of text. Although Library C has had a "mending" unit for years, the supervisor has been left to devise her own procedures without input from the professional staff. Mending "solutions" applied over the years, although often inventive, have created a legacy of inappropriate and damaging repairs throughout the collection. Furthermore, because the heavily used departmental libraries are often without access to any repair services, items are routinely added to the collection without adequate binding or protection.

The Library's director of one year has quietly observed the inadequacy of preservation, conservation, and maintenance activities, and has launched a long range planning effort to develop a comprehensive preservation program for the collections.[1] Because the development of a full-scale program is expected to take several years while funds and new positions are sought, the Library's new Preservation Committee has studied the literature and determined that an effort to improve the Library's maintenance and repair program should begin immediately.

Because of the size and breadth of its collections, Library C needs to implement a wide range of conservation activities. Its *immediate* needs, however, are to discontinue damaging and inappropriate repairs, retrain staff to perform conservationally sound procedures, and increase conservation services to heavily used departmental libraries. Although it would be desirable to institute positive change without alienating the present supervisor of the mending unit, given human nature this may not be possible. Therefore personnel changes may be necessary.

Library C should hire a consultant with extensive experience in collections conservation for a large research collection. This consultant should analyze present activities and prepare a phased plan for *basic* conservation services for the entire library system. The plan should include the upgrading of facilities and equipment as needed. The Library's contract for commercial library binding should also be reviewed at this time. Based on the consultant's report, a conservator should be hired to retrain staff, ideally on a one day per week basis. Such an arrangement would only be possible if a suitable conservator were within reasonable commuting distance from the library. Another alternative would be to arrange for training of the supervisor of the "conservation unit" at a library with an established comprehensive preservation program.

As Library C's new conservation initiative is implemented, a task force composed of several collection development/public services staff should work with the conservation unit supervisor to determine priorities and devise policies for conservation treatment decision making. It would be useful to engage the consultant again at this point to provide input to the work of the task force.

It will take years for Library C to establish a conservation unit capable of meeting all of the needs of the collection. However, many needs can be met immediately by retraining staff and realigning priorities. Adjustments to the conservation program will occur naturally as Library C develops a comprehensive preservation program.

Library D

Library D is a well-supported public library serving a township population of 100,000 with additional users from surrounding rural communities. The library is housed in a Carnegie-era building that is air-conditioned, and has been renovated and expanded. Besides addressing the recreational reading interests and information needs of a largely middle-class community, Library D is heavily used by high school students researching term papers and by the large business community for ready reference. Largely through the efforts of the local historical society, Library D has compiled significant collections in local history and genealogy that are heavily used on a daily basis by enthusiastic senior citizens.

To maintain their fiction collection, much of which quickly becomes outdated, staff at Library D can with good conscience use commercial book repair tapes sold by library supply companies. Selected titles in disrepair deemed to be of long-term interest, and new quality paperbacks should be rebound or recased by a commercial library bindery.

---

[1] Item 7 of the Selected Bibliography outlines a self-study process for libraries developing preservation programs.

Periodicals used by high school students and the business community should also be regularly bound.

Library D can make good use of the "Tightening the Hinges of a Case-bound Book" and "Replacing a Torn Endsheet" procedures for its reference collection and for new books that arrive from the vendor loose in their cases. For reference works that are not superseded, and other items kept on a long-term basis, but not heavily used, Library D might make a modest investment in the supplies required for "New Bookcloth Spine with Mounted Original Spine" and "Recasing Using the Original Cover" procedures. Library D is lucky to have a library assistant of many years who can train part-time high school student assistants to do the work.

Because Library D has a large audiovisual collection, conservation efforts should include the proper maintenance and use of phonograph records, tape recordings, videotapes, and films.

The local history and genealogy collection contains older materials whose main conservation needs are proper storage and handling. "Protective Enclosure Procedures" can be carefully executed by historical society members trained at a workshop sponsored by a regional library network or state historical agency. "Mending Using Japanese Paper and Starch Paste" is also an acceptable technique for novices who have been thoroughly trained. Since surveyor's and city maps, architectural drawings, and other flat paper documents are heavily used, "Polyester Film Encapsulation" should be considered as a method of protecting these items from wear and tear. Selected manuscripts can also be encapsulated. The use of historic photographs should be strictly controlled and copies made of the more popular images to protect the originals.

Because the largest part of Library D's collection is routinely weeded, its major conservation task is to protect items from needless wear and tear so that they are available for use as long as they are needed. For materials that will be indefinitely retained, library staff can make informed decisions about repair and treatment based on their knowledge of the collection and the community.

Appendix 3
Equipment, Tools, Supplies, and Suppliers

EQUIPMENT

Board shear	American Printing Equipment, BookMakers, Ernest Schaefer, Gane Bros., L. Hardy, or used machinery companies
Book press	American Printing Equipment, Basic Crafts, BookMakers, Ernest Schaefer, Gane Bros., Lincoln Wire, TALAS, or custom-made
Corner rounder	American Printing Equipment, Holliknger
Guillotine paper cutter	American Printing Equipment, Gane Bros.
Measurephase™ (book measuring device)	Bridgeport National Bindery
Paper cutter, table-top model	American Printing Equipment, Gane Bros., Lincoln Wire
Phase Box Maker (crimping machine)	Hollinger
Pressing boards, metal-edged	American Printing Equipment, Gane Bros., Lincoln Wire, or custom-made
Rivet fastening machine	TRW Carr Division
Soft Spray® System	Wei T'o®
Stamping press; type; type cabinet	American Printing Equipment, Ernest Shaefer, Gane Bros.
Ultrasonic welder	William Minter
Velo-bind® (paper punch)	office supply company

TOOLS

Artist's oil painting brush	art supply stores

Awls	hardware stores, BookMakers, Conservation Materials, Gane Bros., TALAS
Bone folder	American Printing Equipment, Basic Crafts, BookMakers, Gane Bros., TALAS
Electrician's clamps, rubber tipped	hardware stores
Embroidery scissors	fabric stores, Conservation Materials, TALAS
Glass, ¼-inch plate	local glass supplier
Glue brushes	American Printing Equipment, Basic Crafts, BookMakers, Conservation Materials, S. & S. Brush Manufacturing, TALAS
Japanese utility brush	Aiko's
Japanese water color brush	Aiko's
Kitchen knife	hardware stores
Knitting needles, rigid metal	department stores, yarn stores
Lead weights	metal supply companies, McMaster-Carr, plumbing supply stores
Oven mitt	kitchen supply stores
Oyster knife	kitchen supply stores
Rulers, self-centering	art supply stores
Rulers, stainless steel with cork backing	art supply stores, American Printing Equipment
Sandpaper block	hardware stores
Scalpel	medical supply companies, BookMakers, Conservation Materials, TALAS
Scissors/shears	fabric stores, American Printing Equipment, BookMakers, Gane Bros., TALAS
Squeegee	hardware stores
Spatula	Conservation Materials, TALAS
Staple remover	office supply stores
Straightedge, steel	American Printing Equipment, TALAS
Surgical scissors	Squibb & Sons
T-square	art supply stores, American Printing Equipment

Tacking iron	Brodart, Conservation Materials
Triangle	American Printing Equipment, TALAS
Triangle, self-centering	art supply stores
Tweezers	drugstores, American Printing Equipment, Conservation Materials, TALAS
Whisk, tiny	kitchen supply stores
Yardstick	art supply stores, hardware stores, American Printing Equipment

SUPPLIES

Blotting paper	photographic supply stores, Hollinger, Process Materials, University Products
Bookboard	Conservation Resources, Gane Bros., Process Materials
Bookcloth/buckram	A/N/W, BookMakers, Holliston Mills, JoAnna Western, TALAS, University Products (precut rolls)
Boxboard	A/N/W, Hollinger, Library Binding Service, Process Materials, University Products
Bristol, pH neutral or alkaline, .010, .020, .030	Hollinger, Process Materials, Rinsing Paper, TALAS, University Products
Cambric hinge cloth	fabric stores, Gane Bros.
Double-sided tape, 3M Scotch Brand® no. 415	Conservation Resources, Hollinger, University Products
Endsheets	A/N/W, Hollinger, Library Binding Service, Paper Source, Process Materials, TALAS, University Products
Envelopes, pH neutral or alkaline	Conservation Resources, Hollinger, University Products
Grosgrain ribbon, polyester	fabric stores
Heat-set tissue	BookMakers
Inlays, Archivart® heavy duty library endleaf	Process Materials
Japanese paper	Aiko's, A/N/W, Paper Source, TALAS

Linen thread	Basic Crafts, BookMakers, Conservation Materials, TALAS, University Products
Linen thread, waxed, thick	leather craft supply stores
Magic Rub® erasers	art supply stores, Conservation Materials, TALAS
Map folder stock, .010, .020	Conservation Resources, Hollinger
Matboard, pH neutral or alkaline	Hollinger, Process Materials, Rising Paper, University Products
Nylon cord, braided	fishing supply stores
One-Wipe® dust cloths	grocery stores, hardware stores, Guardsman Chemicals
Polyethylene washers	Conservation Resources, Specialty Bolt & Screw
Polyester film	Conservation Materials, Hollinger, Pilcher Hamilton Corp., University Products
Polyvinyl acetate (PVA) adhesive	Aabbitt Adhesives
Pressboard	Gane Bros., Process Materials, University Products
Remay® (non-woven polyester)	BookMakers, Conservation Materials, TALAS, University Products
Rivets	TRW Carr Division
Sandpaper	hardware stores
Scalpel blades	medical supply stores, BookMakers, Conservation Materials
Sewing needles	fabric stores, BookMakers, Conservation Materials
Silicone release paper	University Products, TALAS
Stamping foil	BookMakers, Gane Bros., University Products
Starch paste	BookMakers, Conservation Materials
Super cloth	fabric stores, BookMakers, Gane Bros.
Waxed paper	food service supply companies, grocery stores, hardware stores

MISCELLANEOUS ITEMS

Cotton rags, soft, clean, lintless
Cutting boards from scraps of bookboard, boxboard, etc.
Empty dish-detergent bottle
Empty one-pound coffee can
Jars for glue
Pressure-sensitive tape
Small bowl or wide-mouthed jar for mixing paste
Wastepaper from endsheets, computer printouts, etc.
Weights, bean bags, wrapped fire bricks, covered laminated bookboard, lead, paper weights, small pieces of ¼-inch
     plate glass

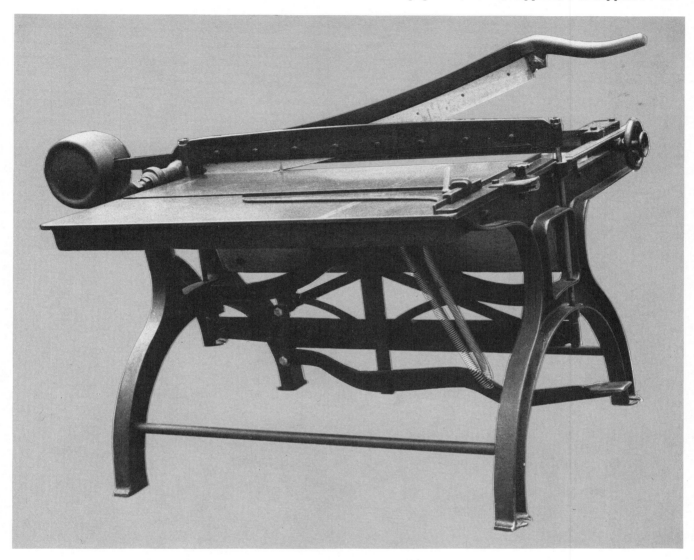

40-inch J. Jacques and Son board shear manufactured around the turn of the century. Jacques® Universal Shears are still manufactured. Other shears are also available. Board shears are the center of the conservation workshop. They are built with adjustable gauges for cutting stock, a foot clamp to hold materials in place, a counterweight to balance the heavy-duty curved blade, and a trash receptacle. The board shear is a very large pair of scissors and should be used to *cut only one thickness of material at a time.* Properly adjusted, the shear will stay sharp for years and will cut both very thin and very thick material. Used shears are sometimes available from used machinery outlets or from commercial binders that have converted to power cutters.

Book press and brass-edged boards for book *repair.* Although this sturdy, simple press is no longer manufactured, many libraries already own models. A similar press can be custom-built (see the following photograph), or a book*binding* press can be used. The "daylight," or opening, of the press determines how many books can be held at one time.

Book repair press designed and built at the Fine Instruments Research Shop, Southern Illinois University at Carbondale.

Standing floor press with very large "daylight." Flat boards have been stacked in the opening so that the press may be used for a relatively small number of books.

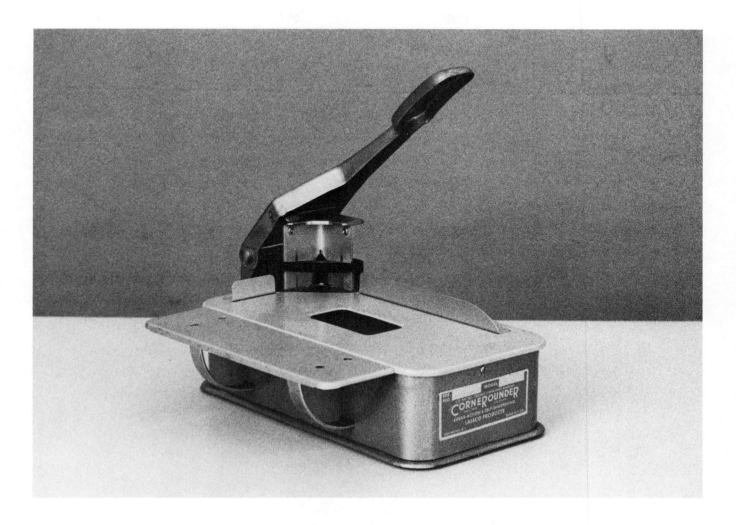

Model 20 Corner Rounder®, Lassco Products, Inc., Rochester, N.Y. A foot-powered model is also manufactured. Interchangeable blades are available to make corners of different sizes.

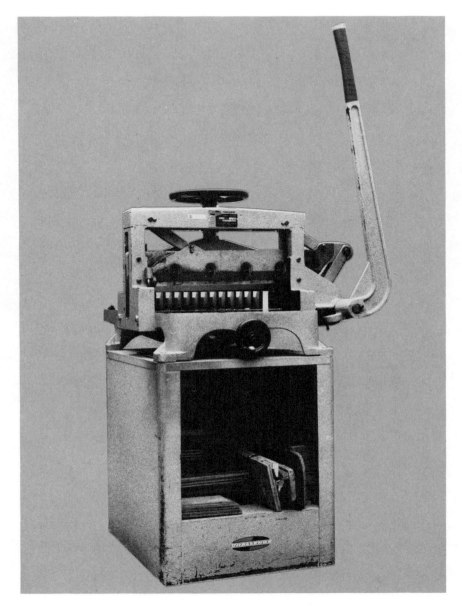

Challenge® Pony Lever Paper Cutter with Steel Stand, Challenge Machinery Company, Grand Haven, Mich. A guillotine paper cutter used for cutting a stack of paper or card stock. This cutter can be used to crimp boxboard by substituting a slightly rounded blade for the hollow-ground cutting knife.

Measurephase™, a device used for quick, accurate measurement of books. The scale on this unit has been adapted to the metric system.

Kutrimmer™, Michael Business Machines Corp., New York, N.Y., a table-top model paper cutter featuring a hand-held clamp to hold materials in place and adjustable gauges for use in cutting. This brand is available in various sizes (size of bed). Several thickness of stock may be cut at one time, the number depending on the model.

Phase Box Maker from Hollinger Corporation, Arlington, Va., used for crimping boxboard.

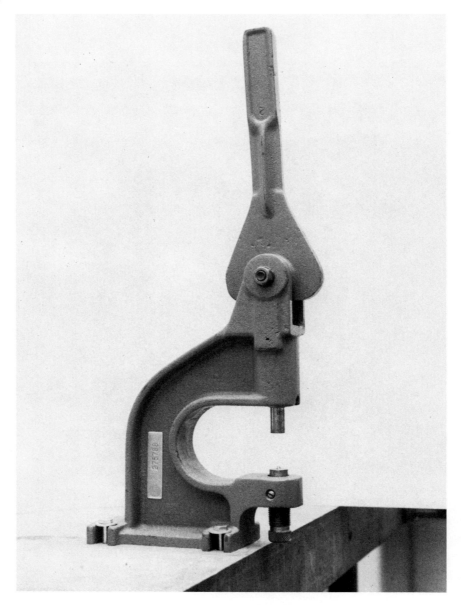

Rivet-fastening machine from TRW United Carr Supply, Rosemont, Ill. This machine is equipped with die no. 9570 and die no. 9114. The rivets used are no. BS 22405 (finish K0300) and no. BS 99972 (finish K030L).

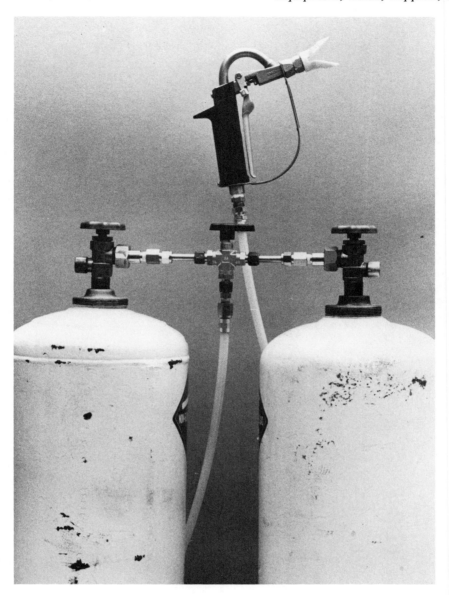

Wei T'o Soft Spray® System for non-aqueous deacidification, developed by Wei T'o Associates, Inc., Matteson, Ill. This system must be used in a fume hood or a spray booth. Detailed instructions for use are available from the manufacturer.

Kwikprint® stamping press, Model 55, Halvorford Kwikprint
Company, Jacksonville, Fla. Pallet and chase adapter for the
press manufactured by Ernest Schaefer, Inc., Union, N.J.

American Brass Type steel type cabinet, American Printing Equipment and Supply Co., Long Island City, N.Y.

Ultrasonic welder for polyester film encapsulation manufactured by William Minter, Chicago, Ill. A smaller version is also available.

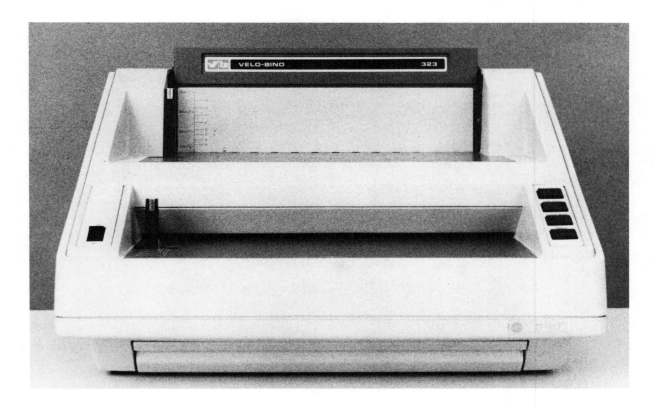

Velo-bind® machine for punching non-tearing holes in polyester film.

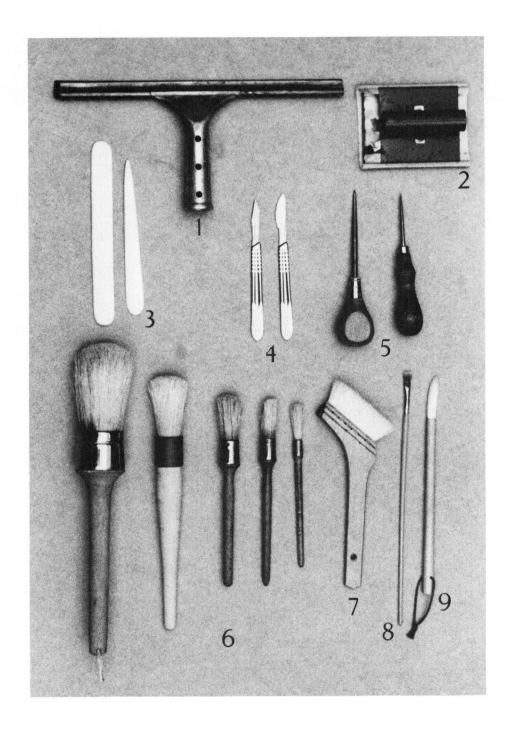

1—Squeegee. 2—Sandpaper block. 3—Bone folders. 4—Scalpels. 5—Awls. 6—Glue brushes. 7—Japanese utility brush. 8—Artists' oil-painting brush. 9—Japanese water-color brush.

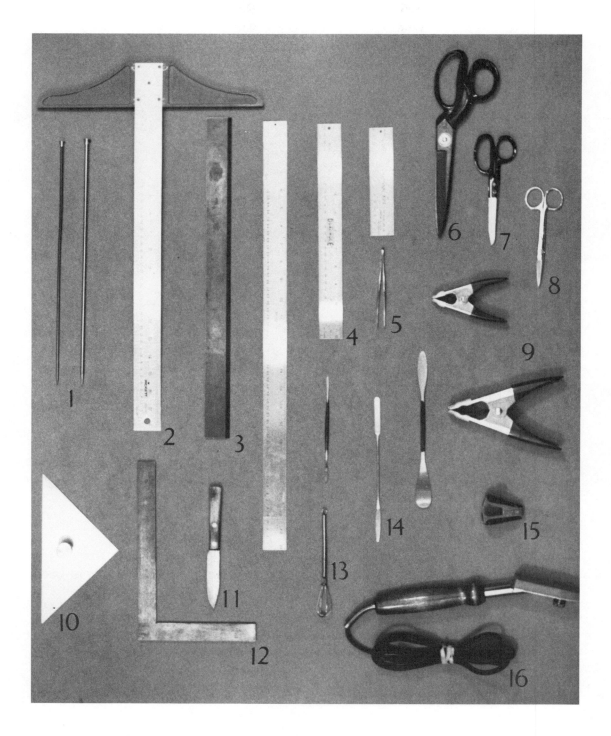

1—Knitting needles. 2—T-square. 3—Straightedge. 4—Rulers. 5—Tweezers.
6—Shears. 7—Scissors. 8—Surgical scissors. 9—Electricians' clamps. 10—Triangle.
11—Kitchen knife. 12—Square. 13—Whisk. 14—Spatulas. 15—Staple remover.
16—Tacking iron.

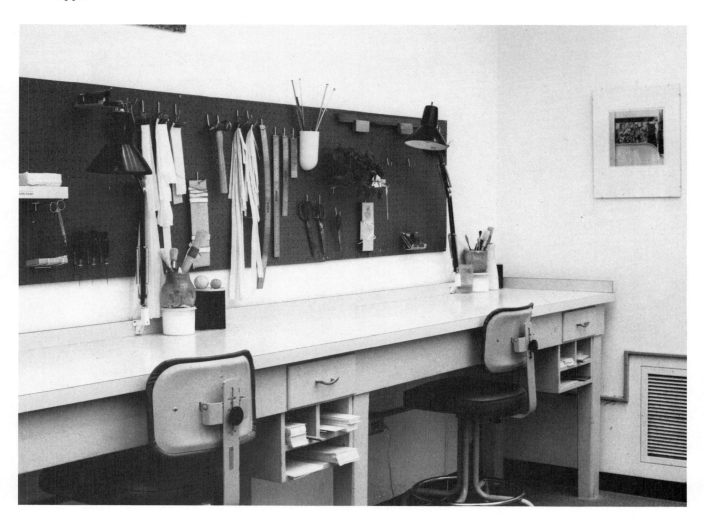

Book Repair Work Bench, Conservation Lab, Morris Library, Southern Illinois University at Carbondale.

This book repair work bench contains individual work stations for routine book repair. The bench is at a comfortable work height so that staff members can stand or sit on swivel chairs with casters. Adjustable incandescent lights provide directed light. All the tools and supplies necessary for book repair are kept at each station. Slots under the drawers hold strips of wastepaper and blotting paper and sheets of waxed paper. The work bench is close to both a board shear and routinely used supplies. Book presses stand on a sturdy table behind the bench. Work-in-progress is stored near the bench on individual shelves, not left at work stations. The formica work surface is easily cleaned. Organized work stations facilitate work flow and productivity by encouraging staff to be neat and methodical.

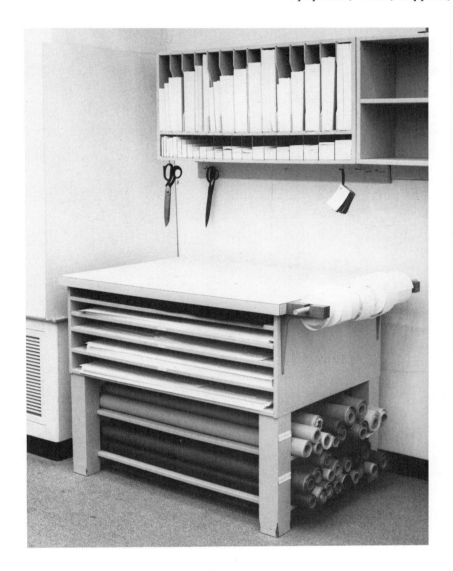

Book Repair Supply Station, Conservation Lab, Morris Library, Southern Illinois University at Carbondale.

A book repair supply station holds materials frequently used by book repair staff and provides a work surface for assembling supplies. (Large quantities of supplies may be kept in more remote locations.) The supply station is a two-part unit. A formica-top table has shelves for folders containing strips of bookcloth, full-size sheets of various endsheet papers, and rolls of bookcloth and buckram. A dowel attached to the side of the table holds rolls of pre-cut super cloth. Attached to the wall above the table is a shelf with slots to hold various sizes and shades of pre-cut endsheets and pre-cut strips for inlays. A yardstick, scissors, bookcloth sample book, and masking tape (for holding bookcloth rolls closed) are always kept at the supply station. Since supplies for book repair are pre-cut and books are batched according to the kind of repair needed, a central supply station reduces the time required to assemble materials, helps to streamline workflow, and contributes to an orderly workshop.

MANUFACTURING COMPANIES AND SUPPLIERS

Aabbit Adhesives
2403 N. Oakley Avenue
Chicago, IL 60647
(312) 227-2700

Bookbinding ethylene vinyl acetate copolymer resin adhesive No. 834-403 (old Jade No. 403)

Aiko's Art Materials Import
714 North Wabash Avenue
Chicago, IL 60611
(312) 943-0745

Sample books available upon request

American Printing Equipment and Supply Co.
42-25 Ninth Street
Long Island City, NY 11101
(718) 729-5779

Andrews/Nelson/Whitehead (A/N/W)
31-10 48th Avenue
Long Island City, NY 11101
(718) 937-7100

Minimum orders
Distributors around the country

Basic Crafts
1201 Broadway
New York, NY 10001
(212) 679-3516

BookMakers
2025 Eye Street, NW
Washington, DC 20006
(202) 296-6613

Samples available upon request

Bridgeport National Bindery, Inc.
P.O. Box 289
104 Ramah Circle South
Aggawam, MA 01001
(413) 798-1981

Measurephase™

Brodart, Inc.
1609 Memorial Avenue
Williamsport, PA 17701
(800) 233-8467

Conservation Materials Ltd.
Box 2884
340 Freeport Boulevard
Sparks, NV 89431
(702) 331-0582

Conservation Resources International, Inc.
8000-H Forbes Place
Springfield, VA 22151
(703) 321-7730

Ernest Schaefer, Inc.
731 Lehigh Avenue
Union, NJ 07083
(201) 964-1280

Gane Bros. and Lane, Inc.
1400 Greanleaf Avenue
Elk Grove Village, IL 60007
(312) 593-3360

Guardsman Chemicals, Inc.
Consumer Products Division
3503 Lousma Drive, SE
Grand Rapids, MI 49508
(616) 247-7651

L. Hardy Company
17 Mill Street
P.O. Box 267
Worcester, MA 01603
(617) 756-1511

Hollinger Corp.
P.O. Box 6185
3810 South Four Mile Run Drive
Arlington, VA 22206
(703) 671-6600

Holliston Mills
P.O. Box 478
Kingsport, TN 37662
(800) 251-0251

JoAnna Western Mills Co.
2141 South Jefferson Street
Chicago, IL 60616
(312) 226-3232

Library Binding Service
2134 East Grand Avenue
Des Moines, IA 50305
(800) 247-5323

Lincoln Wire Co.
42-25 Ninth Street
Long Island City, NY 11101
(718) 784-7010

McMaster Carr Supply Co.
P.O. Box 4355
Chicago, IL 60680
(312) 833-0300

Branches in Atlanta, Dallas, St. Louis, New Jersey, San Francisco, and Vernon, California

distributor for Universal Jacques Shear (board shear)

Sample books available upon request
Minimum orders

Sample books available upon request
Minimum orders

Paper Source
204 West Superior
Chicago, IL 60610
(312) 337-0798

Pilcher Hamilton Corp.   Melinex® 516
2350 South 27th Avenue
Broadview, IL 60153
(312) 343-8100

Process Materials Corp.   Samples available upon request
301 Veterans Boulevard
Rutherford, NJ 07070
(201) 935-2900

Rising Paper Co.   Authorizes distributors
Housatonic, MA 01236
(413) 274-3345

S. & S. Brush Manufacturing Co.
915 Broadway
New York, NY 10010
(212) 260-5959

Specialty Bolt and Screw Inc.   Hi density polyethylene flat washer,
48 Capital Drive   ¾"x.195x.032
Box 519
West Springfield, MA 01089
(800) 322-7878

Squibb & Sons Inc.
Weck Division
2420 South Pasfield Avenue
Springfield, IL 62704
(217) 544-5332

TALAS   Sample books available upon request for a fee
213 West 35th Street
New York, NY 10001-1996
(212) 736-7744

TRW United Carr Supply   Rivet-fastening machine to include: die no. 9570,
10544 West Lunt Avenue   die no. 9114, rivet no. BS 22405 (finish K0300),
Rosemont, IL 60018   rivet no. BS 99972 (finish K030L)
(312) 296-7161

University Products
South Canal Street
P.O. Box 101
Holyoke, MA 01041
(800) 628-1912

Wei T'o Associates, Inc.
21750 Main Street, Unit 27
P.O. Drawer 40
Matteson, IL 60443
(312) 747-6660

Wei T'o Soft Spray® Deacidification System

William Minter Bookbinding and Conservation
1948 West Addison
Chicago, IL 60613
(312) 248-0624

Ultrasonic Welder for Polyester Film
Encapsulation

Appendix 4
Dexterity Test

A simple dexterity test given to prospective employees can help determine if individuals are well suited to conservation work. It can also give those being interviewed an opportunity to see if the work is compatible with their expectations. Although manual dexterity is only one indication of an individual's potential for success in a conservation job, it will directly affect the quantity and quality of their work.

The dexterity test is intended to be straightforward and nonthreatening. To help a prospective employee feel at ease, it can be explained as the equivalent of a typing test for a clerical job. However, even if the person taking the test is nervous, natural dexterity will be apparent.

The test includes operations routinely performed in the conservation laboratory. Operations unfamiliar to the prospective employee are demonstrated by the interviewer.

The test has five parts and takes approximately 10 minutes to administer. Supplies are easily assembled and, if preferred, they may be stored together for convenience.

A. Grain Direction
   After a brief explanation of grain direction and how it is determined, the prospective employee is asked to find and mark grain direction of 15-cm square pieces of paper, matboard, and boxboard.[1]

B. Texture Differentiation
   The prospective employee is asked to determine which of two samples of bookcloth is the thickest. Given a sample of matboard, he/she is asked to indicate the more textured side.

C. Manipulation of Tools
   The prospective employee is asked to:
   1. Cut a straight line through a piece of paper with a small pair of scissors.
   2. Water-tear a strip of Japanese paper after a demonstration by the interviewer.[2]
   3. Punch a hole in a piece of boxboard with a 1/8-inch punch and hammer.

D. Judgment
   The prospective employee is asked to:
   1. Draw a circle, any size
   2. Give a 5 cm measure, estimate 3 mm, 6 mm, and 3 cm.
      _____ 5 cm
   3. Using a straightedge, draw a parallel line 6 mm in from the right edge of a letter-sized piece of paper.

E. Manipulation of Materials
   After seeing a demonstration by the interviewer, the prospective employee is asked to:
   1. Fold a sheet of paper in half, twice, using a bone folder.
   2. Remove a piece of paper floating in water from a photographic tray and transfer it to a drying rack.

---

[1]See item 36 of the Selected Bibliography for a discussion of grain direction.
[2]See step 3, page 105, "Mending with Japanese Paper and Starch Paste."

3. Apply paste to a piece of paper and attach it to a piece of bookboard.
4. Apply glue to a piece of bookcloth and attach it to a piece of bookboard.

To evaluate dexterity, the interviewer should consider the following aspects of the prospective employee's performance on the test:

1. Was the person reasonably accurate? Was he able to determine grain directions and textures of the samples? How accurate were the estimates of length?

2. Did the person follow directions well? When a procedure was demonstrated, did the prospective employee mimic the motions exactly, or immediately forget what was shown? Was the person able to complete the procedures from start to finish without prompting? Did the person easily understand what was expected of him?

3. Did the person handle the tools confidently or tentatively? Did the person move quickly and smoothly, or awkwardly? Did the person hold the hammer securely and give a strong rap? Did the person paste or glue neatly?

The skills of the interviewer, including intuition and the ability to communicate, will determine the usefulness of the dexterity test in predicting job success and aptitude for conservation work. A good performance on the test does not ensure success if a person's attitude toward the work is bad. Someone who seems nervous during the test may truly want the job and might perform well if hired. On the other hand, someone who performs quickly or in an offhand manner might be just as quick to leave if not quite pleased with the job.

The person responsible for the hiring should administer the dexterity test, or at least observe it, rather than relying on another's judgment. Although personal prejudices may enter into evaluations, awareness of one's *own* prejudices can help in making adjustments so as not to obscure the potential of a prospective employee.

Appendix 5
Glossary

ACID DETERIORATION: Degradation of a material such as leather or paper from the chemical effects of acids. Acids may be present in library materials because of their original manufacture, through contact with air pollutants, or by migration from acids in adjacent materials.

ACID MIGRATION: Movement of acids to adjacent materials, causing staining, weakening, and embrittlement. *See also* ACID DETERIORATION.

ADHESION: The joining of two materials by the application of an intervening substance such as glue or paste.

ADHESIVE BINDING: A method of attaching single book leaves together to form a text block by applying a flexible glue to the spine; developed to avoid the expense of sewing sections together to form a text block. Also called PERFECT BINDING. Double-fan adhesive binding using a slow-drying POLYVINYL ACETATE (PVA) ADHESIVE can be quite durable. However, a HOT-MELT GLUE is impermanent and forms a rigid spine which rapidly deteriorates.

ALKALINE: A designation of the acid content using the pH scale where 1 is most acidic and 14 is most basic. A paper with a pH above 7.0 (neutral) is alkaline. Most paper products used in conservation contain an alkaline buffer to guard against future acid formation by absorption of air pollutants. Paper with an alkaline reserve generally contains 1-3% calcium carbonate as a buffer and measures 8.5 on the pH scale. The terms "acid-free" and "archival" are frequently used instead of alkaline.

ANIMAL GLUE: A glue consisting of proteins derived from "cooking" animal materials such as hides and bone. Warmed animal glue dissolved in water is tacky and viscous and forms a strong bond when it dries. Animal glue will deteriorate over time, becoming hard and brittle and losing its adhesive qualities. The term "glue" is often used instead of the general term "adhesive." *See also* POLYVINYL ACETATE (PVA) ADHESIVE, STARCH PASTE, and HOT-MELT GLUE.

ATTACH(MENT): To glue or paste together.

BASE/BASEBOARD: The bottom board of a box or portfolio, usually the exact size of the item being enclosed.

BIBLIOGRAPHIC INTEGRITY: The retention of original physical components, STRUCTURE, and FORMAT.

BLIND STAMP: An impression made by a tool without using stamping foil. *See* STAMPING FOIL.

BLOTTING PAPER: A soft, unsized paper board used to absorb moisture.

BOLT: 1) A length of woven cloth as it comes off the loom (with two finished edges, the SELVAGE); 2) The untrimmed folded edges of book sections.

BONE (the action of boning): Two remove air bubbles, smooth, flatten, and ensure adhesion between two materials by rubbing with a flat tool made of bone or plastic, which is called a bone folder or folder.

BOOK: 1) A published work, usually printed on paper and protected by a cover; 2) The text block and its endsheets, linings, and cover.

BOOKBOARD: A thick, machine-made paperboard produced especially for bookbinding and consisting of layers of pulp pressed into flat, smooth sheets. The thickness is usually expressed in caliper inch, e.g., .082 inch. Has a definite GRAIN DIRECTION. Also called binder's board.

BOOKCLOTH: A thin, woven cloth like muslin that has been dyed, impregnated with starch (starch-filled), and subjected to heat and pressure.

BOOK RETURN/DROP: A destructive, but widespread, method of returning circulated books, where books are dropped into a box by way of a slot or slide. Called by many euphemisms, the resulting damage is the same.

BOXBOARD: Layered paperboard, similar to artist's MATBOARD, designed specifically for conservation uses. The surface of boxboard is finished so that it does not require a COVERING MATERIAL.

BRISTOL: Thin paperboard with a smooth surface. Used for lining the spine of a cover (the INLAY), and for construction of pockets or small PORTFOLIOS.

BRITTLE: A weakened condition of paper due to ACID DETERIORATION. In extreme cases, brittle paper breaks off when it is flexed or lifted. Frequently accompanied by darkening of the paper.

BUCKRAM: A coarse woven cloth like canvas that has been dyed, impregnated with starch (starch-filled), and subjected to heat and pressure. Buckrams are frequently coated with pyroxylin or acrylic and used for commercial LIBRARY BINDING.

BURST BINDING: An adhesive binding method in which slits are cut through the folds of each section and adhesive applied to the spine of the text block in such a way that the adhesive is forced through the slits, attaching all leaves together. Many new bindings may appear to be SMYTH-SEWN when they are actually ADHESIVE BOUND.

CAMBRIC: A closely-woven, starch-filled cloth used for HINGING.

CASE: The finished COVER of a CASE-BOUND book.

CASE-BOUND: A modern binding method where the text block and cover are made separately and attached in an operation called CASING-IN. Case binding differs from traditional hand bookbinding where the text block and cover are constructed as a single unit. In a traditional "bound" book, leather covers are laced to the text block by the sewing CORDS. Not all leather books are "bound," however; many 19th century imprints covered in leather are case bindings.

CASING-IN: Attaching the text block to its cover, usually by gluing or pasting the super and endsheets, placing the cover around the text block, and pressing until dry.

CHAIN LINES: The widely spaced parallel lines visible when a sheet of handmade paper is held up to the light. Chain lines are watermarks made when the chain wires on the papermaker's mold displace paper fibers. Chain lines can be produced on machine-made paper, in which case the GRAIN DIRECTION of the paper is usually parallel to the chain lines.

CLEAT SEWING/LACING: A machine method of ADHESIVE BINDING developed to use less inner margin than OVERSEWING. Thread covered with glue is laced around large notches cut out of the spine.

COATED PAPER: A slick, glossy paper originally developed for superior reproduction of half-tone screens, but also used for many other printing purposes because it can be printed with great ease. Also called "art paper" or "clay-coated" paper. Coated paper is difficult to successfully adhesive bind because adhesives do not readily penetrate the coating to adhere to the paper fibers.

COCKLE: 1) Wrinkling or puckering caused by uneven drying of paper; 2) The shrinking of stretched paper as it dries.

CONSERVATION: 1) Maintaining in usable condition; 2) The action (especially treatment) taken to stabilize the condition of an item or return it to usable condition. *See also* PRESERVATION.

CORDS: Pieces of hemp or linen twine around which SECTIONS are sewn. The ends of the cords are laced into the COVER BOARDS. Cords appear as the raised bands on the spine of a hand-bound book. Fake cords were frequently built into 19th century cases. *See also* TAPES.

COVER: The outer protection of the text block. In a hard cover book, the cover extends past the edges of the pages. *See also* SQUARE. The cover of a paperback or pamphlet is usually made of heavier paper stock than the text block and is cut flush. Also called CASE.

COVER BOARDS: Rectangular pieces of matboard, pressboard, or bookboard used in the construction of a cover for a book or the outer cover of a portfolio or box.

COVERING MATERIAL: Paper, leather, bookcloth, buckram, or synthetic bookcloth used as an outer covering for hard cover books or protective boxes.

CREASE: A line made by applying pressure to a pliable material. Usually not as distinct as a FOLD.

CRIMP: Compression of fibers along a line before bending to facilitate bending or folding.

DEACIDIFICATION: See NEUTRALIZATION AND ALKALINE BUFFERING.

DEPTH (of a book): The measure of a book at its thickest point including the covers.

DETERIORATED/DETERIORATION: Degradation of a material; loss of physical qualities or impairment of intended function.

DISTRIBUTE (type): Return individual pieces of TYPE to their proper spaces in a type cabinet. To facilitate retrieval, the letters should all face to the left in the cabinet.

DRY: To allow the moisture (usually from gluing or pasting) to leave a material while the material is held or pressed in a desired configuration.

DURABILITY: The retention of strength of a material; its ability to resist wear and tear.

EDITION: All copies of a work printed from the same printing plates and bound in the same manner.

ENDSHEETS: Protective/decorative papers (usually with a single fold) attached to the front and back of a book to protect the text and help hold the book in its cover. In better bindings, endsheets are sewn together with the sections. Also called endpapers, end leaves, or board papers. *See also* FLY-LEAVES.

FLAP: A part of a portfolio that folds over the enclosed item to hold it in place without shifting.

FLAT BACK BINDING: A binding without the characteristic curved SPINE produced when the text block is ROUNDED AND BACKED. A flat spine encourages the text block to sag away from its cover. Almost all paperbacks are flat back as, unfortunately, are many large, hard cover art books. Also called square back.

FLY LEAVES: 1) Blank leaves at the beginning and end of a book; 2) The free (unattached) part of the endsheets that helps to protect the text block.

FOIL: *See* STAMPING FOIL.

FOLD: To bend something over onto itself, as to fold in half.

FONT: A set of TYPE of the same size and design. A font can include letters, punctuation, and numerals. Fonts for hand stamping are typically sold with either lower case or upper case letters.

FORE-EDGE: The front edge of a book; the side opposite the SPINE.

FORMAT: The physical form of an item and the way its component parts relate to one another. *See also* STRUCTURE.

FRAGMENTS: Portions of an original binding that may be retained for their HISTORIC VALUE following FULL CONSERVATION TREATMENT given to a valuable item.

FULL CONSERVATION TREATMENT: Extensive physical treatment given to an individual item with acknowledged intrinsic value. The item's origial component materials and present condition are typically documented and subsequent treatment detailed. *See also* FRAGMENTS and PHOTODOCUMENTATION.

GRAIN DIRECTION: The dominant direction of PAPER FIBERS in a machine-made paper. Paper bends, folds, and tears most easily in the direction of the grain. The grain direction of all of the paper materials in a book should run parallel to the SPINE.

HARDBOUND/HARDBACK: A book whose protective cover is constructed of bookboard covered with bookcloth, paper, etc.

HEAD: The top of a book as it sits upright.

HEIGHT (of a book): The longest dimension of a book as it sits upright on its TAIL. Synonymous with LENGTH.

HINGE: 1) The part of the cover that fits down into the SHOULDERS made when the text block is ROUNDED AND BACKED; 2) The space left between the cover boards and the spine; 3) A paper stub or guard attached to a loose plate, or the folded edge of a plate that allows it to be sewn into a binding along with the sections; 4) The part of the SUPER that extends beyond the edges of the spine and is used to attach a book to its case.

HINGE AREA: The part of a binding joining the text block to the cover. *See also* JOINT.

HISTORIC VALUE: 1) The interest that a book or binding has beyond the information transmitted by its printed words; 2) The integrity of a book in terms of its original production details and accidents of time. *See also* BIBLIOGRAPHIC INTEGRITY.

HOT-MELT ADHESIVE: A resinous adhesive which is liquid when hot and solid when cool. Produces a bond almost immediately on contact with a cool surface such as the spine of a text block. Hot-melts are used extensively for binding PAPERBACKS. They are not suitable for books that will be ROUNDED AND BACKED because the glue becomes stiff when cool. In addition to being relatively inflexible, hot-melt adhesives are not PERMANENT.

IN-HOUSE: On the premises of a particular library.

INLAY: A piece of thick paper or lightweight BRISTOL attached to the COVERING MATERIAL between the COVER BOARDS; exactly corresponds to the width of the spine of the text block.

INNER MARGINS: The inside, blank edges of book pages that are exposed when the book is opened. When the sections of a book are intact (untrimmed), the inner margins are exposed to the fold, and the book, if bound properly, will lie open easily. A properly made ADHESIVE BINDING also exposes the entire inner margin without damage to the binding. When alternate methods of sewing, such as side-sewing or oversewing, intrude upon the inner margins, the book is hard to read, awkward to hold open, and difficult to photocopy. The total inner margin on facing pages is sometimes called the "gutter." See also OVERSEWING.

INTRINSIC VALUE: Historic, bibliographic or artifactual value of an individual item that is dependent on the retention of its original parts.

JAPANESE PAPER: A traditional handmade paper of great variety, versatility, and charm. Produced in the provinces/villages of Japan. Known for its properties of flexibility, strength, and PERMANENCE. Papers commonly used in conservation and bookbinding include Goyu, Hosho, Sekishu, Kizukishi, and Tengujo.

JOINT: The point at which the cover boards pivot as the book is opened. *See also* HINGE and HINGE AREA.

LEAF/LEAVES: The individual pages of a book.

LEAFCASTING: A mechanical method of mending paper documents by filling in voids and damaged areas with compatible paper fibers. A leafcasting machine is used to deposit fibers evenly in a slurry called PAPER PULP.

LEATHER-BOUND: A book covered in leather. Leather prepared by vegetable tanning was commonly used as a covering material for books until about 1820. Leather produced since about 1700 is more subject to deterioration than earlier leather. Because of the flexibility of leather, it can be glued directly to the spine of a text block. This type of binding is known as "tight back" as opposed to CASE-BOUND.

LENGTH (of a book): *See* HEIGHT (of a book).

LIBRARY BINDERY: A commercial enterprise that binds books using mass production methods. The Library Binding Institute is a trade association that sets standards for the library binding industry.

LIBRARY BINDING: A bookbinding produced in an assembly-line fashion with the assistance of power machinery.

LININGS: Cloth and paper attached to the SPINE of the text block to help the book keep its shape. *See also* SUPER and SPINE STRIP.

MACHINE-SEWN SECTIONS: A group of folded sections (gatherings, signatures) that are sewn together through the fold on a machine. The sewing is not "all along" the section like hand sewing; multiple threaded needles spaced at equal distances pierce the folds of individual signatures to attach them together by a chain stitch. *See also* SMYTH-SEWN.

MAINTENANCE: 1) Action taken to keep materials in usable condition; 2) Storage and shelving practices that help materials stay in good condition. *See also* PREVENTATIVE MAINTENANCE.

MATBOARD: A layered paperboard traditionally made from all-rag fiber and used in the framing of works of art or photographs. Thickness is measured in layers or "plies": 2-ply, 4-ply, 6-ply. Used for many conservation purposes and no longer exclusively composed of rag fibers. (Note that rag fiber does not automatically imply ALKALINE.) Alkaline matboard is now available in several shades and colors.

MECHANICAL DAMAGE: Damage caused to a book by physical manipulation in storage, handling, or use. Includes internal movement caused by rapid fluctuations in humidity and temperature.

MENDING: Realigning torn edges of an item, usually by adding a support not intrinsic to the object, such as a strip of paper or cloth. *See also* REPAIR.

MICROENVIRONMENT: Atmospheric conditions inside an enclosure. A microenvironment usually acts as a buffer against outside changes in temperature and humidity and protects against most air pollutants.

MIXTURE (of PVA and starch paste): A combination of POLYVINYL ACETATE (PVA) ADHESIVE and STARCH PASTE; results in an adhesive combining the fast drying and strength of PVA with the working qualities of paste.

MOUNT: To attach something on top of a base material, usually by means of an intervening substance such as glue.

NEUTRALIZATION AND ALKALINE BUFFERING: Synonymous with "deacidification." Conservation treatment that acts chemically to stabilize paper against ACID DETERIORATION. Involves neutralizing acids present in the paper and buffering to leave an ALKALINE reserve to guard against future acid attack, especially from atmospheric pollutants. Common parameters of treated paper are a pH of 8.5 and an alkaline reserve of 2-3%. "Deacidification" will not strengthen already weakened paper. There are a variety of manual methods used by conservators, including aqueous and nonaqueous (solvent) methods where the deacidification agent is applied by immersion, brushing, or spraying as well as mass deacidification methods applied to a quanitity of books in a vacuum chamber.

NOTCHING: A method of preparing a spine for ADHESIVE BINDING that involves cutting thin slits of variable width and depth into the page edge, thereby increasing the surface area in contact with the adhesive. Particularly useful in conjunction with the double-fan adhesive binding method used by library binderies.

OPENABILITY: The ease with which a book opens to display its contents. Primarily influenced by shape of the spine and the method of page attachment.

OVERSEWING: A method of machine sewing employed by the LIBRARY BINDING industry. Thin groups of loose pages are attached together by the piercing action of multiple threaded needles. Results in a very strong attachment. Drawbacks to oversewing are intrusion on the inner margins, the destructive action of the needles perforating the pages, and a condition called "mousetrapping," where a book springs shut if it is not held open firmly. Oversewn volumes do not open flat for photocopying and brittle paper will break off at the point of sewing.

PAMPHLET: A book composed of less than 100 pages (typically) and usually given only a paper cover. *See also* SINGLE-SECTION.

PAPERBACK: A book that has a flexible paper cover. Usually it is also adhesive-bound. Paperbacks with sewn sections can be given hard covers while still retaining their through-the-fold format. *See also* ADHESIVE BINDING.

PAPER FIBERS: The cellulose fibers that make up a sheet of paper or the layers of BOOKBOARD or MATBOARD.

PAPER PULP: 1) The raw material of paper made from macerated cellulosic materials; 2) Paper fibers suspended in water which are used to form a sheet of paper.

PERFECT BINDING: *See* ADHESIVE BINDING.

PERMANENCE: The stability of a material and its resistance to chemical deterioration.

PHASED CONSERVATION: A concept developed at the Library of Congress by conservator Peter Waters and colleagues. Phased conservation was originally conceived to meet the short-term needs of items that would eventually be given FULL CONSERVATION TREATMENT. Surveying is an important aspect of phased treatment: items are categorized by certain characteristics or conservation problems so that they may later be retrieved for treatment.

PHOTODOCUMENTATION: Photographs taken before, and sometimes during, the treatment of a valuable item to document the original structure and component materials.

PHYSICAL ITEM: A book in terms of its structure and construction.

POLYVINYL ACETATE (PVA) ADHESIVE: An internally plasticized copolymer adhesive that dries quickly and remains flexible over time. Results in a very strong bond. PVA is not a REVERSIBLE adhesive.

PORTFOLIO: A protective enclosure with flaps that hold the enclosed item in place.

PRESERVATION: The action taken to retard, stop, or prevent deterioration by providing a proper storage environment, policies for handling and use of library materials, conservation treatment for damaged or deteriorated items, and selective transfer of deteriorated items to an alternative format such as microfilm.

PRESERVATION MICROFILMING: Replacing or reformatting an original by photo-reproduction of the text. Microfilming that produces an archival copy (the original is discarded after filming) involves following national standards to prepare the text (collating and eye-legible targets) and following technical standards for film type, production, processing, and storage of the master negative. The bibliographic control of items preserved by microfilming is important in order to avoid duplication of preservation efforts among libraries.

PRESS: To apply even pressure on an item until it is dry; to encourage it to conform to a desired shape. *See also* DRY.

PRESSBOARD: A stiff, slick cardboard or thick coated BRISTOL.

PRESSURE-SENSITIVE TAPE: An adhesive tape that attaches to a surface when pressure is applied. Unfortunately, the adhesive on tapes frequently used to mend paper eventually deteriorates, leaving a sticky brown residue which stains and embrittles the paper.

PREVENTATIVE MAINTENANCE: 1) Anticipation of potential damage and the steps taken to prevent it; 2) Provision of treatment to protect an item from damage or deterioration in the future.

PROTECTIVE ENCLOSURE: A custom-made enclosure, such as an envelope, folder, portfolio, or box that protects an item from dust, light, mechanical damage, and most air pollutants.

PUBLISHER'S BINDING: Mass production bookbinding for duplicate copies of the same printing of a work. Very economical because each binding has exactly the same dimensions, format, structure, and component materials. Also called EDITION binding.

PYROXYLIN BOOKCLOTH/BUCKRAM: Bookcloth that is given a plastic coating or finish to resist wear and tear. Commonly used in the LIBRARY BINDING industry. Because of pollution generated during manufacture, pyroxylin cloth is gradually being replaced by acrylic-coated cloths.

REBINDING: Giving a book a completely new binding, including resewing or reattaching the pages, new END-SHEETS and spine LININGS, and a new COVER. In library binding, rebinding often means trimming the SECTIONS and OVERSEWING; in hand bookbinding it means repairing the sections and sewing through-the-fold.

RECASING: 1) Reattaching a book to its original cover without disturbing the sewing or method of page attachment; 2) Replacing the original cover with a new cover without disturbing the original page attachment.

REPAIR: To remedy damage done to an item, usually by adding new material to replace damaged or deteriorated material. *See also* MENDING.

REINFORCE: To strengthen an item by adding support material.

REVERSIBLE: A principle of sound conservation treatment whereby whatever is done to an item can be undone, or the treatment reversed, without further damage to the item.

RIVETS: Metal parts used to join two materials. Consists of two parts that are hammered or clamped together.

ROUNDING AND BACKING: A bookbinding operation that gives a book its characteristic curved SPINE. Rounding controls the distribution of swelling from the sewing threads and forms a convex spine that prevents the book from sagging forward. Backing forms a SHOULDER for the edges of the COVER BOARDS to fit against. *See also* FLAT BACK SPINE.

RUB: To smooth, using the fingers or a soft cloth.

SECTION: A group of consecutive pages formed when a printed sheet of paper is folded. The outside folds (BOLT) are trimmed leaving the center, or inside, fold intact. Consecutive sections are sewn through-the-fold to form the text block. Also called signatures or gatherings. "Signature" originally referred to a letter or numeral placed at the bottom of the first page of each printed sheet of paper to assist in collating the book. Modern books are collated by a diagonal solid line across the spine. *See also* MACHINE-SEWN SECTIONS.

SELVAGE: The finished outer edge of a woven fabric. The selvage runs parallel to the warp threads (GRAIN DIRECTION) of the fabric.

SEWING OVER TAPES: A method of sewing where the sections are sewn through-the-folds and the sewing thread passes around tapes (usually three to five tapes) on the outside of the folds. The tapes are then glued onto or laced into the cover, helping to strengthen the attachment of a book to its case. Tapes are most often used in hand bookbinding, although some through-the-fold machine sewing may be done with tapes. *See also* MACHINE-SEWN SECTIONS.

SHOULDER: The outer edge of the curved SPINE against which the boards fit. Made when a book is ROUNDED AND BACKED. *See also* HINGE and JOINT.

SINGLE-SECTION: An item (usually called a pamphlet) that is composed of a single group of folded pages.

SMYTH-SEWING: A method of sewing through the center folds of sections. Named for the inventor of the first practical through-the-fold book sewing machine. See also MACHINE-SEWN SECTIONS.

SPINE: 1) Of the cover—The space between the COVER BOARDS which accommodates the thickness of the text block or the depth of an item being enclosed in a box or portfolio. The spine of a cover is usually stiffened with BOOKBOARD or BRISTOL and stamped with the author and title. A HINGE left on either side of the spine allows movement of the cover boards as the book or box is opened and used; 2) Of the text block—The back or folded edges of a group of sewn sections or the glued edge of an ADHESIVE BINDING. Usually ROUNDED AND BACKED, glued, and lined with cloth and paper.

SQUARE: The part of the cover that extends beyond the edges of the text block to protect the pages.

STAMP: To make a printed impression on a cover by using heated type pressed onto colored foil and into the covering material. *See also* STAMPING FOIL and TITLING.

STAMPING FOIL: Coated polyester film that is placed between hot type and covering material for stamping. The film is coated, or laminated, on one side with atomized metals such as gold or aluminum and comes in rolls of various widths. Pigmented or colored foils are much cheaper than metal foil and thus widely used.

STARCH PASTE: An adhesive made from wheat or rice starch mixed with water. Will last only two or three days without refrigeration. Paste used for bookbinding and conservation usually contains a substance to discourage insect infestation.

STOCK: 1) Supplies bought in large quantities or sizes to realize a cost saving; 2) Basic materials kept on hand from which a variety of items can be constructed or assembled.

STRUCTURE (of a binding): The physical form of a book binding and the interrelation of its parts. Includes such aspects of binding as the method of sewing or page attachment, the shape of the spine, the method of attachment of text block to cover, endsheet construction, etc.

SUPER: A woven cloth that is glued to the SPINE of the text block. The excess that extends past the ends of the spine (usually 2-3 cm) is used to attach the book to its case. Also called "mull" or "crash."

SYNTHETIC BOOKCLOTH: An imitation bookcloth used by the LIBRARY BINDING industry as a covering material for book bindings. Frequently used as an alternative to buckram for covering material.

TAIL: The bottom of a book as it sits upright.

TAPES: Strips of woven linen around which sections are sewn. *See also* CORDS and SEWING OVER TAPES.

TEXT BLOCK: The group of sections or leaves that form the book before it receives its cover.

TIPPED ONTO/TIP-ON: Attachment of an item along one edge by the application of a thin line of glue.

TITLING: Printing the name of the author and the title of a book on the cover or a protective box by using a stamping press. The press holds and heats the type that leaves the printed impression in the cover. *See also* STAMP.

TRAY: An uncovered box with three sides or walls and no top. In the construction of a double-tray box, the inside and outside trays fit together to enclose the item.

TRIM: To cut away the excess not needed for the construction of an item or to reduce bulk.

TURN IN: To fold over, or fold to the inside, the raw edge of materials producing a finished edge. The material folded over is typically called the "turn-in."

TYPE: A rectangular piece of metal with one letter, numeral, etc., in relief on the top surface. Individual type is set into a press for stamping. Also called "letters."

WARP: A bend or distortion caused by unequal pressure on one side of a material. Usually happens when paper or bookcloth is moistened (expanded) and attached to only one side of a piece of board. Warp also occurs when a material such as leather or vellum shrinks in an overly dry environment. Warping can also occur when the GRAIN DIRECTIONS of attached materials are not parallel to one another.

WATER TEAR/TORN: Tearing PAPER FIBERS along a moistened and creased line to produce a soft, feathered edge.

WEIGHT: To apply even pressure on an item that is drying. *See also* PRESS.

WIDTH (of a book): The widest part of a book from the outside curve of the SPINE (or raised bands on the spine) to the front edge (fore-edge) of the COVER BOARDS).

Selected Bibliography

1. American Institute for Conservation of Historic and Artistic Works. **Code of Ethics and Standards of Practice.** Washington, D.C.: American Institute for Conservation, 1979.

    A professional code of ethics for practitioners treating cultural objects. Describes the obligations of the conservator to the object, to the profession, and to the public. Codifies guidelines for examination and treatment, scientific analysis, and reports and contracts.

2. Boomgaarden, Wesley. "Preservation Planning for the Small Special Library." **Special Libraries** 76, no. 3 (Summer 1985):204-11.

    Describes a planning strategy for preservation programs for small libraries and suggests priorities.

3. Brown, Margaret, Donald Etherington, and Linda McWilliams. **Boxes for the Protection of Rare Books: Their Design and Construction.** Washington, D.C.: Library of Congress, 1982.

    Instructions for making boxes for rare books, including specifications, construction techniques, diagrams, and materials. Includes a phased preservation box, portfolio, fore-edge grip box, and standard rare book box. Compiled in the Preservation Office at the Library of Congress.

4. Callery, Bernadette, and Jean Grunner, comps. **Guild of Book Workers Supply List.** New York: Guild of Book Workers, March 1985.

    Based on information received when the membership was surveyed, this 82-page pamphlet contains a supplies index, a geographical index, and a list of suppliers. Available for $12.50 from the Guild of Book Workers, Inc., 521 Fifth Ave., New York, NY 10175.

5. Clarkson, Christopher. "The Conservation of Early Books in Codex Form: A Personal Approach." **The Paper Conservator** 3 (1979):33-50.

    A landmark discussion of the philosophy and ethics of conservation treatment of rare books.

6. Council on Library Resources. Committee on Preservation and Access. **Brittle Books: Reports of the Committee on Preservation and Access.** Washington, D.C.: Council on Library Resources, 1986.

    A summary of four years of work to develop a strategy for a nationwide program to solve the brittle book problem. Introduces the committee's successor, the Commission on Preservation and Access, whose mission is to organize and plan an ongoing program and raise funds for preservation.

7. Darling, Pamela W., and Duane E. Webster. **Preservation Planning Program: An Assisted Self-Study Manual for Libraries.** Washington, D.C.: Association of Research Libraries, Office of Management Studies, 1982.

    A self-study guide to using staff "study teams" to assess preservation needs and plan a program for a specific institution. ARL will provide consultants for libraries desiring a formal "assisted self-study." New edition forthcoming in 1987.

8. DeCandido, Robert. "Preserving Our Library Material: Preservation Treatments Available to Librarians." **Library Scene** 8, no. 1 (March 1979):4-6.

   Discusses options in the physical treatment of a hypothetical library volume, including do nothing, discard, replace, commercially bind, provide a storage container, encapsulate individual pages, or restore. Article demonstrates a practical approach to conservation treatment decision making.

9. Frost, Gary. "Conservation Standard Rebinding of Single Books: A Review of Current Practice at the Newberry Library." **AIC Preprints** (1977):56-61. Paper presented at the 5th annual meeting of the American Institute for Conservation of Historic and Artistic Works.

   Presents a philosophy for treatment of a seventeenth-century printed book (poorly rebound in the nineteenth century) as a prototype in the development of conservation rebinding procedures. Outlines steps and techniques and the principles behind them and highlights crucial areas and conflicts.

10. Godden, Irene P., and Myra Jo Moon. **Organizing for Preservation in ARL Libraries.** Washington, D.C.: Association of Research Libraries, Office of Management Studies, Systems and Procedures Exchange Center, July-August 1985. (SPEC Kit No. 116).

   Includes resources culled from ARL libraries that pertain to the organization of preservation departments and activities within libraries. Includes an excellent short overview of patterns of organization.

11. Greenfield, Jane. **Books: Their Care and Repair.** New York: H. W. Wilson, 1983.

   A manual of book repair and protective enclosure procedures that includes a useful chapter on setting up a workshop. Illustrated with the author's line drawings.

12. Gwinn, Nancy, ed. **Preservation Microfilming: An Administrative Guide** [tentative title]. Chicago: American Library Association, forthcoming, 1987.

   A complete guide to the state of the art of preservation microfilming. Includes chapters on major issues such as selection of materials, bibliographic control, preparation for filming, standards and practices, and costs. An appendix covers guidelines for contracting out the actual filming.

13. Haines, Betty M. "Deterioration in Leather Bookbindings—Our Present State of Knowledge." **British Library Journal** 3, no. 1 (Spring 1977):59-70. See also discussion in **Abbey Newsletter** 2, no. 3 (December 1978):28.

   Explains the reasons behind leather deterioration, including tanning methods, air pollution, and types of skins. Discusses solutions to deterioriation.

14. Harry Ransom Humanities Research Center, Conservation Department, University of Texas at Austin. **Conservation Supplies and Suppliers.** Chicago: American Library Association, Resources and Technical Services Division, June 1984.

   In response to a request from ALA's Preservation of Library Materials Section, the Conservation Department at HRC made their in-house list of conservation supplies and sources available for distribution. The list is arranged by subject and appendices include material specifications. Available for $5.00 from ALA/RTSD, 50 E. Huron St., Chicago, IL 60611.

15. Hazen, Dan. "Collection Development, Collection Management, and Preservation." **Library Resources and Technical Services** 26, no. 1 (January/March 1982):3-11.

   Describes the types of decisions required by preservation and suggests structures and criteria. Discusses the importance of preservation's interface with collection development.

16. Horton, Carolyn. **Cleaning and Preserving Bindings and Related Materials.** 2d ed. rev. Chicago: American Library Association, 1969. (Library Technology Program Publication, No. 16).

   Includes specific procedures and techniques in the reconditioning, repair, and protection of library materials. The appendices list supplies, sources, and equipment.

17.   Illinois Cooperative Conservation Program. **A Simple Workstation for the Conservation of Library Materials.** Carbondale, Ill.: Illinois Cooperative Conservation Program, September 1984.

A 10-page pamphlet describing equipment, tools, and supplies for conservation, including plans for a simple workstation. There is a brief explanation of the use of each item listed and an inset lists sources. Available free from ICCP, c/o Morris Library, Southern Illinois University, Carbondale, IL 62901.

18.   Koda, Paul. "The Analytical Bibliographer and the Conservator." **Library Journal** 104, no. 15 (1 September 1979):1623-26. (LJ Series on Preservation, No. 6).

Discusses the areas where the work of the analytical bibliographer and the conservator overlap, including their attitudes towards physical details, documentation, and the ethics of treatment. Advocates cooperation between the professions, development of interdisciplinary standards for recording information, and improved awareness through publication and workshops.

19.   Kyle, Hedi, et al. **Library Materials Preservation Manual.** New York: Nicholas Smith, 1983.

Includes a series of simple, clever enclosures that can be constructed by the novice. Contains good working tips on measuring, pasting, clean-up, etc. Separate section on setting up a work area and supplies and equipment.

20.   Lehmann-Haupt, Hellmut. "On the Rebinding of Old Books." In **Bookbinding in America: Three Essays.** rev. ed. New York: R. R. Bowker, 1967. [Originally published in 1941.]

Philosophical discussion of the rebinding of old books. Introduces the idea of a "conservation rebinding" where permanent materials and methods are more important than the "fineness" of the work.

21.   Library Binding Institute. **Library Binding Institute Standard for Library Binding.** 8th ed. Rochester, N.Y.: Library Binding Institute, 1986.

A completely revised edition of a trade standard for library binding incorporating many of the concerns of libraries for bindings that enhance preservation. Addresses the issue of alternatives to oversewing as the primary method of leaf attachment used by library binders. Includes technical and materials specifications and a glossary. Available for $5.00 from LBI, 150 Allens Creek Rd., Rochester, NY 14618.

22.   Library of Congress. National Preservation Program Office. "County Atlas Project." **National Preservation News,** no. 2 (October 1985):8-9.

Describes a long-term project to provide conservation treatment for LC's collection of over 1,600 county atlases. The atlases were treated by an outside contractor who followed LC specifications for deacidification, repair, encapsulation, and binding. Specifications are available from the National Preservation Program Office.

23.   Library of Congress. National Preservation Program Office. **Handling Books in General Collections.** Washington, D.C.: Library of Congress, 1984.

A 10-minute slide/tape presentation on the proper storage and handling of library books. Suitable for training library staff. Available for loan or sale.

24.   Library of Congress. Preservation Office. **Polyester Film Encapsulation.** Washington, D.C.: Library of Congress, 1980. (LC Publications on Conservation of Library Materials).

A pamphlet describing LC's rationale for polyester film encapsulation, including a discussion of the properties of polyester film and the effects of encapsulation. Drawings illustrate the technique of making a polyester envelope and encasement of a folded item. An appendix recommends specific instructions for ordering and lists manufacturers and sources of supply.

25.   Merrill-Oldham, Jan. "Binding for Research Libraries." **The New Library Scene** 3, no. 4 (August 1984):1, 4-6.

Guidance for librarians in choosing a binding method and especially a page attachment method appropriate for particular volumes.

26.   Merrill-Oldham, Jan. "Method of Leaf Attachment: A Decision Tree for Library Binding." **The New Library Scene** 4, no. 4 (August 1985):16.

A decision-making flowchart intended as a supplement for item 25 above.

27.   Merrill-Oldham, Jan. **Preservation Education in ARL Libraries.** Washington, D.C.: Association of Research Libraries, Office of Management Studies, Systems and Procedures Exchange Center, April 1985. (SPEC Kit No. 113).

Includes materials on preservation education programs in ARL Libraries for library staff, readers, and potential donors and senior administrators.

28.   Merrill-Oldham, Jan, and Merrily Smith. **The Library Preservation Program: Models, Priorities, Possibilities.** Chicago: American Library Association, 1985. Proceedings of a conference held 29 April 1983.

This conference, the first in a four-part series, includes papers from libraries with established preservaton programs. The contents are especially useful for their emphasis on planning and fiscal concerns. This conference preceded a period of greatly expanded preservaton program development in research libraries and is notable for its descriptions of model programs.

29.   Milevski, Robert J. **Book Repair Manual.** Carbondale, Ill.: Illinois Cooperative Conservation Program, July 1984.

Developed in conjunction with a series of hands-on workshops, this manual includes instructions for 10 simple book repairs including an excellent discussion of "quick and dirty" repairs for adhesive bindings. Also included are a list of the contents of the "ICCP Book Repair Kit"; a list of tools, supplies, and sources; and sources for endsheet paper. For those organizations interested in holding workshops, kit specifications are included, with costs. Available for $5.00 from ICCP, c/o Morris Library, Southern Illinois University, Carbondale, IL 62901.

30.   Morrow, Carolyn Clark. **The Preservation Challenge: A Guide to Conserving Library Materials.** White Plains, N.Y.: Knowledge Industry Publications, 1983.

An overview of the preservation problem and preservation program development in the United States. Includes case studies of preservation programs and a chapter with contributions from conservators. An appendix contains ample job descriptions.

31.   National Archives and Records Service. **Intrinsic Value in Archival Materials.** Washington, D.C.: National Archives and Records Service, 1982. (Staff Information Paper No. 21).

A landmark publication that concisely describes those characteristics of a document or group of documents that dictate retention in original format—versus preservation by reformatting. Includes three examples of the use of the concept of intrinsic value as applied by the National Archives.

32.   Parisi, Paul. "Methods of Affixing Leaves: Options and Implications." **The New Library Scene** 3, no. 5 (October 1984):9-12.

Written by the president of a binding company, a technical description of page attachment methods listing major advantages and disadvantages of each.

33.   Rebsamen, Werner. "Acid-pHree Binder's Board: A Reality." **The New Library Scene** 3, no. 6 (December 1984):13-16.

Discusses the implications of using alkaline materials in library binding and describes the manufacture of binder's board.

34.   Rebsamen, Werner. "Endpaper Construction for Recasing." **The New Library Scene** 4, no. 1 (June 1985):15-18.

Technical description of several methods of constructing and attaching endpapers that relates them to the overall construction of the text block.

35. Rebsamen, Werner. "Hot-Stamping Foils." **The New Library Scene** 5, no. 1 (February 1986):14-16.
Describes the development, manufacture, and use of decorative foils and discusses qualities of permanence.

36. Rebsamen, Werner. "Paper Grain." **The New Library Scene** 4, no. 1 (February 1986):13-16.
Describes the importance of machine grain direction in paper products and the implications for the text block and the binding. Lists six methods for testing grain direction.

37. Ritzenthaler, Mary Lynn. **Archives and Manuscripts: Conservation, A Manual on Physical Care and Management.** Chicago: Society of American Archivists, 1983. (Basic Manual Series).
An excellent overview of conservation management in archival institutions. Appendix B includes instructions for basic conservation procedures.

38. Roberts, Matt T., and Don Etherington. **Bookbinding and the Conservation of Books, A Dictionary of Descriptive Terminology.** Washington, D.C.: Library of Congress, 1982. (A National Preservation Program Publication).
The primary source for basic information on preservation and conservation. Terms are described fully with many cross-references and notations to the bibliography for source definitions. Beautifully illustrated.

39. Shahani, Chandru. "To the Editor ... [Encapsulation Research]." **Abbey Newsletter** 10, no. 2 (April 1986):20.
A clarification of LC research on the effects of encapsulation on the aging of a document inside an envelope.

40. Walker, Gay, et al. "The Yale Survey: A Large-scale Study of Book Deterioration in the Yale University Library." **College and Research Libraries** 46, no. 2 (March 1985):111-32.
A full description of a three-year project to study book condition at Yale. Outlines the survey methodology and results for 15 distinct library collections.

41. Wessel, Carl J. "Deterioration of Library Materials." **Encyclopedia of Library and Information Science**, edited by A. Kent and H. Loncour, 7:60-120. New York: Marcel Dekker, 1972.
Beginning with a thorough discussion of the historical background of deterioration research, this article goes on to explain deteriorative forces: environmental factors (light, humidity, heat, and air pollution); biological agents; and acidic components in library materials. Detailed and containing many references to previously published research.

42. Williams, Lisa B. "Selecting Rare Books for Physical Conservation: Guidelines for Decision-making." **College and Research Libraries** 46, no. 2 (March 1985):153-59.
A discussion of a rationale for conservation treatment decisions for rare books that consider factors such as monetary, intellectual, and aesthetic value and projected use. Describes a study in selection conducted at the University of Chicago.

43. Young, Laura. **Bookbinding and Conservation by Hand: A Working Guide.** New York: R. R. Bowker, 1981.
A comprehensive manual of hand bookbinding techniques for the fine binder. Especially useful for the chapters "Equipping a Workshop," Materials and Their Use," and "Finishing."